DRIVEN
MY WORDS, MY TRUTH

Fight for what they said you couldn't have

Bryant Lavender

#8

To: Courtney Isgett

It was such a pleasure to have met you.
It was even more awesome to find out You
were writing a book. Don't stop, God placed
that book in your belly to spread the word.
Be obedient, Confident, and excited.
Greatness is inside of you, I pray the words
on these pages spark and add fuel to your
fire. Go walk into your destiny!

DRIVEN
MY WORDS, MY TRUTH

Fight for what they said you couldn't have

Bryant Lavender

Published by CreateSpace

Cover photography by Stephanie McNeill
Editorial and marketing services, DWilson & Associates, LLC

Printed in the United States of America

ISBN: 978-1987480214

Visit www.bryantlavender.com

ACKNOWLEDGMENTS

God

He gave me the idea to write this book. Through prayer and sensitivity to the Spirit, He gave me the words, gave me the content, and He chose the direction of this book. Thank you, Lord God for using me to reach your people. Thank you for every trial and tribulation I went through to get me to this point.

Dorothy Wilson

Thank you for being an amazing editor, for pouring your expertise into me and being encouraging through everything to get me to this point. You took the time to ensure this manuscript of my life was done in a professional way. Most of all, you cared. Thank you for taking a motherly role and guiding me to be a better author as well as being a better young man.

Coach McNeill "Coach Coe"

Thank you for your constant pushing, coaching and concern. Thank you for listening to God's divine assignment with me. The bond that we have only gets stronger as the years go by. Thank you for sowing a solid foundation into me. The insight you've given me, prepared me for the sports world. Thank you for being that one coach in high school who believed in me from the start and for never being afraid to tell me when I was wrong. You never let me get too high or too low, but always showed love.

Vernel Champ

Thank you, my brother, for being friendly, for having that calm spirit about everything. You always brought the cognitive thinking to the forefront. Thank you for being an awesome friend in a time of my life when I still was unsure of myself and of who I was in God. Thanks for being the encouragement on the field whether it was over a catch, a drop, or an executed or missed assignment. My brother, I needed that.

Tre Donald

Thank you, my brother, for being my competition and calling me out. Your ways constantly made me self-evaluate. Your challenging spirit fed me what I needed at the time I needed it. I did not want to hear it, but when I look back at the situations that occurred, you were on time for those moments.

Coach Joe Simp

Thank you for having a pure spirit and pushing me to maximize my reps. That lesson was not just between the lines but was outside of them as well. I know you say I earned my opportunities to play, but it was because you followed through that everyone had an opportunity. Thank you for being detailed, nitpicky and questioning, because it stretched me to the limit so I could be molded into the player and the man I wanted to become.

Coach Dean

Thank you for taking a chance on me and listening to Coach Coe. I still do not think you understand the magnitude of what you did that day (you know the one). You know I often play back the events as to what happened, and now that I am older, I understand. Your assignment with me was over, and God had given you another one. I am forever grateful.

Coach Stone

Thank you for allowing me to represent the University of South Alabama. It was a true honor to wear the red, white and blue. Thank you for the mental pruning. It caused me to seek God more and man less. That was the best lesson I could have ever gotten at that time. Thank you for being the necessary catalyst in that area of my walk with Christ.

CONTENTS

INTRODUCTION

This book had to be written because my story will help encourage you not to just settle for ordinary, because you are extraordinary.

It seems at every step of my life, there was someone telling me I couldn't accomplish my dreams. They would try to encourage me to do something else or introduce me to something that had little or nothing to do with the dreams that were incubating in my heart. I just got tired of hearing, "That is not going to work," "You can't do that," so I took every negative thing anyone has ever said to me and I held onto it, putting it in my gas tank for fuel.

When God planted in my heart the idea of writing this book, I was afraid. Afraid I wouldn't be able to do it or do it well. I was scared, because this was not poetry or some made-up story. This is my story, my testimony, and in this book, you will read my unedited thoughts while I was in the midst of the fire.

I know there are many other people who need to know and believe they can and will accomplish the impossible in their lives.

CHAPTER 1

Prophesy
Speak To Your Situation Regardless of How It Looks

I PROMISE YOU

It was the first week of my first-ever football season, and I was so excited. I slept wearing my whole uniform. I had dreams of making plays, getting hit and just having fun with my friends. The previous year, my Mom had said I couldn't play, because I was too little. The whole time leading up to that season I kept thinking, "Mama! I'm not little anymore. I can play football just like Marques." I had watched my older brother the whole year, studying his moves and the way he ran with the ball. Momma asked me, "What position do you want to play?" "Running back," I answered without hesitation. Marques played that position so it was really the only one I knew. Plus, I saw that he got the ball the majority of the time.

As it turned out, the big first game day wasn't really about the ballgame. The players had to be at the field at least an hour before kickoff time, so Dad came to pick me up around 9:45 a.m. for the Saturday game, but the game was canceled because of the weather. Instead of going back home to Mom's place, I asked Dad if I could go to his house, not realizing that a moment I'd never forget was soon to unfold. "What do you want to do?" he asked. "Nothing, I want to watch the football games coming on and eat some of that good ole popcorn you make," I replied. "OK, that's fine," he said. "Make sure you let your Mama know."

When we arrived at Dad's apartment, I kicked off my shoes and went straight to turn on the TV. I switched to the first college football game that was on. Dad got in the kitchen, pulled out the big iron skillet and got to work making popcorn the old-school way. It took dad about 15 minutes to cook the popcorn and to put it in the big white bowl we always munched out of. As I fixed my eyes on the screen, I locked in on the running backs for each team. Alabama was playing Michigan. I watched both backs for two drives and then walked over to Dad and said, "Daddy, that's going to be me." He chuckled and said, "OK, Bryant." "Daddy, for real, I'm going to play on TV," I said insistently. My father smiled and responded, "OK, son, I hear you."

The look I was giving my Dad could not have been more serious. At age 8, I already knew what I wanted to do and be in life. From that point on, I watched as much football as I could on a daily basis. I just could not get enough, and I set out to be the best football player I could be.

FIVE YEARS LATER

Boom! Boom! Boom! I woke up to someone beating on the front door. I could hear my stepfather yelling, "Who is it, and why are you knocking on my door this early?" I turned and glanced at the clock. It said 5:45 a.m. "Mel, who is it?" my Mom asked, as she got up and headed into the living room. Then there was silence, an awkward silence for what seemed like several minutes but actually was just a few seconds. I heard a faint sentence that ended with "has died." I wasn't sure if I had heard that correctly. My brothers were moving in their beds by now so I couldn't hear clearly. I shook both of them, "Wake up!" I said. "I think someone died." I got up, threw on some shorts and a T-shirt and went to see what was going on.

As I reached the end of the hallway, I could see a man sitting on the couch. He looked to be in his mid-40s. His hair was in different shades of gray; his face was smooth except for his goatee, which was nicely trimmed. He saw me and his eyes seemed to get big for a split second. When they refocused, his face went blank. I looked slightly to the right and saw my Mom's back. "Mama, what's wrong?" My Mom kept crying, and Mel didn't answer, either. He just shook his head. I saw the man had a badge on his hip. I looked him in the eye and asked, "Mr. Detective, what happened? Can you please tell me what happened?" He looked at me with his blank face, swallowed and said calmly, "Well, son, your father has been murdered."

My heart sank. After about 20 seconds of mentally digesting his words, I exclaimed in disbelief, "Argh! I just saw him ... I talked to him on the phone he taught me everything about sports...Daddy!" Tears rolled down my cheeks. "Son, I know you are really good, too," the policeman said, referring to my football playing, as he got up to leave.

The rest of that day was a blur to me. My brothers and I were supposed to have spent the night at my father's house that weekend, but he had told us, "Not this time. You can come next weekend." We did not know that would be the last time we would see him. We listed his address on school registration papers so we could attend nearby Bayou View Middle School. We saw him every day after school. He would take us to practice and to games. His casino job's schedule allowed him to be available at that time.

I remember the last day we ever saw him. It was a Friday afternoon after school. The ride home was one of the best times we had had together. We were laughing, joking and having great quality time together. As we pulled up to our house, Dad put the car in park.

We got out of the car still laughing and joking. When we looked back to say good-bye, he stuck his head and left arm out of the window and yelled, "I love y'all!" "Love you, Daddy!" we yelled back in unison as we opened the door and walked into the house.

December 6, 2003, is the day my father was pronounced dead. Marques was 15, I was 13 and Za'Cari was 10. Everything moved in slow motion for the next few weeks for all of us. During that time, my Mom came home one day from running errands to get the funeral arrangements together. She sat us down for a family meeting. "We have to go view the body, to verify that it's your Dad," she said. "I wanna go," I blurted out immediately. "Nah, Bryant, you don't need to go. That is not something a kid should see." I remember being angry and confused during that time. I was struggling to process my feelings about what was going on.

My father's best friend contacted us to let us know to come get what we wanted out of my father's apartment or everything would be thrown away. As soon as Mel got home from work, we hopped in the van and headed to the apartment. When we got out of the car, Mom gave each of us an industrial garbage bag. When we opened the door, we paused, because it still looked like a crime scene.

Mel, Mom and my brothers walked into the apartment, but I didn't move. I just looked inside the doorway. I saw a Kenwood speaker right inside the door; it was as tall as I was. On top of that was my father's glass ashtray. As I scanned the rest of the room, everything was out of place. There was no clear way to walk. Jet magazines were scattered everywhere, pots and pans were all on the floor, and all the furniture was removed from the wall. As I looked down at my feet before I took a step into the apartment, I saw droplets on the floor. I blinked twice to make sure my eyes were not fooling me. The droplets were blood, and there were a lot of them. They were in a trail, so I followed them, drop after drop. They went from the front door through the living room into the hallway, left into the kitchen, out of the kitchen and into the bedroom. It was a disaster in the bedroom. There were papers everywhere; the closet was open all the clothes were on the floor. The nightstand was flipped over with the drawers pulled out. The mattress was laying on the floor. In the middle of the mattress, there was a massive blood stain. Just to the right of the stain was a small first-aid kit. "He tried to patch himself up," I thought.

I turned around to follow the trail of blood again. It went back into the hallway, past the kitchen into the bathroom. The bloody trail led out of the bathroom into the living room and to the couch where Dad always sat. The couch cushion was turned face down, so I tried to kick it with my foot, but it didn't move. I bent down and pulled it up with my hands. "Man, why is this cushion so hard to pick up?" I thought as it was coming up off the floor.

When I finally got it up, I saw that the bloody trail stopped here. The cushion was soaked in my father's blood. The blood was still damp, and because there was so much, it made the cushion stick to the ground like glue. I flipped the cushion out of the way and just stared at the blood.

"Bryant, take that bag down to the car and come back with another one," my Mom said. "Yes, ma'am," I replied. But before I complied, I looked back at the drying puddle of blood, and I stuck my shoe in it. I just figured that I could take some with me. As I shut the front door to the apartment, it finally hit me that I would never see my father again. I would never physically be close to him again. A tear began to trickle down the left side of my face as I continued to walk to the car to get another trash bag.

That is all I remember from that night. Two days later, it seems everything started to get crazy. The phone began to ring off the hook from people we didn't know. I could see my mom starting to break down. Mel was doing his best to keep everyone level-headed, but I could tell he was getting tired as well. Watching my Mom go back and forth with the funeral home, I could see was taking a toll on her. I wanted to help, but I did not know what to do. I missed my father so much that I started calling his cell phone just to hear his voice on the answering machine. We had such a close bond; I don't know if anyone understood how close we were. The days we hung out, we talked about all kinds of things. I tried to grab as much from him as I could when we were together.

But I still had so many more questions to ask him, so many more experiences I wanted to have with him. I prayed to God to give me one more day with him. I just wanted to give him a big hug with my face on his belly. I just wanted to kick it with my best friend one more time. I had no idea that when I went to sleep that night my prayer would be answered.

DREAM

It was a Saturday, and as usual I was playing video games. I loved playing NCAA football on dynasty mode. I heard what sounded like a knock on the door, but I did not get up to answer because I wasn't sure if it was just noise. I mean, I did have the television kind of loud. "Knock, knock, knock!" I heard it on my window that next time and jumped because it scared me. "Open the door!" I heard my father's voice roar through the window.

I put the video game on pause and got up to open the door. As I walked, I was puzzled. Dad rarely came over without calling first. I guess he was bored and wanted to see me. So, when I got to the door and opened it, I said, "What are you doing here?" "I can't come see my son?" he said with a laugh. I laughed as well as he walked inside. He reached out to give me a hug, but I stepped back, falling to the ground and curling up in the fetal position. I yelled, "No! You are dead!" He gave me a sarcastic look, "I know, Bryant." "Oh," I replied, and got up from the ground and gave him the biggest hug I could. My father was 6-feet, 4-inches tall and at age 13 my head only reached his stomach. I buried my head into his belly. I missed him so much. I tried to wrap my arms around his big frame before we began to wrestle a little bit. After we settled down from roughhousing, we did what we always did during the time we spent together. We watched football for a few hours and then we switched to watching movies. We were hanging out like nothing had ever happened. When it got dark outside, I knew he would be leaving soon.

Before he left, I asked, "Daddy, will you tell me where you were shot?" He looked at me and had the most pleasant look on his face. "Here," pointing to his right side. "Here," pointing to his right arm, and "here," pointing to the right side of his head. He then stood up and said, "Bryant, it is time for me to leave, Son." "I know, Daddy," I responded. I gave him a smile, stood up with him and gave him another huge hug before he left.

"As a man thinketh, so is he." -- Proverbs 23:7

Time to process/recondition your thoughts

1. Has God given you a dream about what
    you will do or has someone else spoken
    see you doing? Write about it.

2. Have you lost sight of your dream because
    of a tragedy, disappointment or even
    negative words spoken about you?

3. How can you use that setback to fuel your
    success?

CHAPTER 2

Fight

Take the Hits, Remember the Dream

REALITY

The wake and the funeral were the following week. Because of the dream about Daddy, I was anxious to see what he would look like in the casket. How would his body that no longer had his spirit in it look? I wondered. To see his body that I had grown to love motionless, void of life, would be tough. I was so nervous. Oh, man, I loved my father. On December 11, 2003, my family and I arrived at the funeral home around 6 p.m. for the wake. Several people were already there. I was really surprised at the number of people. I saw faces of people I just didn't expect to be there.

We began to greet everyone and thanked them for coming. Just before the funeral home attendants opened the room where the casket was, my cousin, Kelvin, and my two best friends, Bernard and Dallas, showed up, and I thanked them for coming.

"Ladies and gentleman, the body for Terry Lavender is now able to be viewed," the attendant announced. I shot to the door. "Somebody get Bryant!" I heard my Mother yell, but it was too late. I had already made it to the casket. I looked at his hand and saw a small X in between the index finger and thumb. I touched his hand, and it was hard and cold. "Daddy! Daddy! Daddy!" I yelled out in a hysterical voice, crying at the same time. A couple of men grabbed me to pull me away. I fell limp and wailed loudly for my father as they carried me outside of the funeral home to try to calm me.

My Dad's best friend talked to me for about 30 minutes before I started to gain my composure. He went inside to get my brothers so we could head to the New Orleans airport to pick up my aunt. She had flown in from California. That temporarily took my mind off of what was happening inside the funeral home.

The funeral was held the next day. I had an awkward feeling as we got into the limo. "Bryant, please don't act a fool like last night," my mother said. "We are not trying to deal with that today. OK?" I noticed that my mother's face was tired. She was grieving and still in disbelief. "Yes, Ma'am," I replied. Everything seemed to be moving in slow motion as we drove to the funeral home. I felt numb inside, as though I was looking at myself from a distance. I was so immersed in my thoughts about how life would be different from then on that I did not realize we had pulled up to the funeral home.

"Come on, Bryant," my stepfather said. I got out of the car and saw so many people. I did not know my father knew so many people. I felt like the whole city of Gulfport, Mississippi, was in there.

I observed people paying their respects differently as they viewed my father -- some were crying, and others just looked at him. When there was a break in people coming to see him, I walked up to the casket one last time. Everyone paused for minute to see what would happen, because they knew how I had behaved the day before. I looked at him from head to toe. I just replayed everything I remembered about all the times we had spent together. All the football talks we had had. How he had tried to be in our lives more the last two years of his life. I glanced over at my Mom, and she had her face in her hands. I guess she thought I was about to lose control, but I kept it together. Turning back to my father, I said, "Daddy, I love you, and I will miss you. I promise I will make it to the NFL, no matter what. When I get there, I am going to get down on one knee and say, 'I made it.'" With tears flowing freely down my face, I said goodbye to the body of my father.

The following week I went to church, searching for hope to fill the void I felt inside. I wanted to know more about God and why He would let my father be killed. That ended up being one of the best days of my life. The Sunday school teacher was talking about love. He explained there are three different ways to love someone: Eros, Philos and Agape. Eros love is love that somebody would have for their spouse. Philos love is love somebody would have for their friend or buddy. The last one, Agape love, is unconditional. That love is what God shows us regardless of what we have done or been through. When he explained what Agape love was, I wanted to experience that type of love from God, and I wanted to be able to give that type of love. When I got home that day, I was still thinking about that. Before I went to sleep, I closed my eyes to pray. "God, what is this Agape love that he was talking about? I want to know this love. If you show me this Agape love, I promise I'll always hold on to you." That declaration I made to God at age 13 was a turning point in my life. It was a most significant marker.

"As a man thinketh, so is he." — Proverbs 23:7

Time to process/recondition your mind

1.   What difficult times have you gone through in life?

2.   What positive, affirmative declaration or promise did you make to yourself?

3.   Say it to yourself again; recommit yourself to it.

CHAPTER 3

Bounce Back
Setbacks Happen; Keep Pushing

SOPHOMORE YEAR

Three years later, I was in the 10th grade and could play varsity football. Not many sophomores get that opportunity, but I felt I had earned it. That is when I met Coach Coe for the first time. He was an intimidating man, for sure.

"Name, number and pants size?" he said when I walked up to him to receive my equipment. "Dang, he has a deep voice," I thought, before replying, "Lavender, 20, and small." As I waited for him to hand me the equipment, I watched his mannerisms. I also wondered where he had played ball and what position he had played. He returned to the window and said, "Here you go. Now you better take care of your equipment. Make sure you take out the dang pads when you put them in the basket for the wash because if I have to, you will be sorry and practicing without them." I stared at him bugged-eyed. "Yes, sir."

I walked away feeling as if I had just gotten chewed out for nothing, even though he was just giving me a warning. I was afraid of Coach Coe, and I was going to do everything I could to stay out of his way. I had worked hard enough to earn second string on the depth chart at the Y position. Bank was first string, so I watched him like a hawk. Everything he did, I did, or he made me do. "You don't understand what I'm doing right now but you will," he would say. Most of the time I didn't know why he was making me do certain things, but he made it a point to be around me. Even when I didn't want to practice, he came to get me and made me.

When Coach Lute came on at Gulfport High, everything changed. He came in like a fireball, ruffling a lot of feathers. I liked that he did it his way. In previous years, we had run a pro-style offense, but now we had switched to a spread offense. That year, I was mainly a special teams guy, relieving Bank when he needed a breather. Sometimes, I was allowed to keep playing to gain experience.

Finally, it was scrimmage day. Bank walked up to me and asked, "You ready?" "Yeah, I'm ready, bro," I replied. "A'ight, we 'bout to see," he said, walking away to converse with the upperclassmen. About five minutes later Coach Lute came in and said, "All right, men, it's time to get it on. Everybody is fully dressed in 15 minutes."

As I dressed, I started to get nervous because this was the start of the journey to establish myself as a playmaker. After dressing, I walked out of the field house and saw the stands were filled. I just smiled at all the support from the city. I felt adrenaline course through my body. I was amped up!

The first period of the scrimmage involved special teams. I was on the kickoff, punt, punt return and field-goal block teams. We were separated into two teams so everyone could have plays on film. I was on the blue team and we had the first possession. The first play was all hitches. "Ready⬜ set ⬜ hit!" I came off the ball fast, ran my three big, two little turn, and I saw the ball coming. I threw my hands up. Drop. That is how most of the night went for me. I saw the ball, put my hands up and I would drop the ball. My morale was so low; I couldn't believe that my debut was going that badly. The quarterback came up to me, and I just shook my head. "You're all right," he said. "I don't know why I can't catch the ball right now," I told him. "I don't know what I am doing wrong." "Relax, you are doing everything fine," he said. "Just catch it. When you see the ball just catch it. Don't worry about anything else, just catch it. I'm still going to throw you the ball, so just catch it." He patted me on the shoulder and walked away. He was right I just needed to just catch the ball. But Coach Coe had seen enough of me dropping the ball. "You keep dropping the ball," he said, "your butt won't play on Friday night!" "Come on, bro," I thought. "Catch the dang ball, man. You trying to play or do you want to ride the bench?"

We lined up on the ride side. This time, we were running all go routes across the board. "Ready . . . set . . . hit!" I exploded off the ball, ran past the second level of defenders and looked for the ball over my left shoulder. I located the ball, took three more steps before leaping into the air and throwing my hands up. That time I came down with the ball. "'Bout time," I said to myself. I knew my performance had hurt my chances of getting playing time for the season. I still had a lot of work ahead of me if I wanted to establish myself as a reliable target for my quarterback. I had that plus more to prove to the coaches. They needed to see that I was ready to play at that level. For the first half of the season, most of my playing time was on special teams. We were playing Pascagoula when I finally got my opportunity to get offensive snaps. "Bryant, you're in," Coach Lute said. It was midway through the third quarter. It was third down and seven yards for the first down. Coach called all slants. "Ready ⬜ set ⬜ hit!" The quarterback fired the ball to me. "Catch it. Catch it. Catch it," I thought. Here it comes. I threw my hands up, and as soon as my hands touched the tip of the ball, boom! I was hit at the same time, and I dropped the ball. I jogged off the field after we punted the ball away. "You had a chance to make a big play for your team, and you let them down," Coach Lute said. "I'm waiting for you to show everyone that you are a player. I thought you were ready. I guess I was wrong." I had no response for him. I just went and sat down on the bench. Bank walked over and said, "B, you good, bro. Everyone drops balls. I even drop balls." "But you don't drop as many as I do," I replied, as I lifted my head to look into his eyes. "You think I got this good overnight?" he said. "It just means we have to put more work in." I nodded my head in agreement.

The following week I was switched to defense. I did not like the change but knew I wasn't cutting it on offense. Plus, some of our defensive backs were down because of injuries. I was athletic enough to play defensive back and was there just in case another one went down. I did become a starter on kickoff, and I had been producing there, so I was happy about that. My third week on defense another defensive back was injured, and I was the next one to step up. I was nervous, because I didn't have that much experience on the defensive side of the ball. I also was 5-feet, 9-inches tall, weighed 142 pounds, and that didn't give me much confidence out there on an island at the cornerback position.

George County was our next opponent and I went to the starting defensive backs for technique help. I wanted to do the best I could for my team. It was one of the hardest games I had played because I just felt uncomfortable out there on an island. We went to a man-to-man defense and I was guarding their best wideout. He was just too fast for me to keep up with. Luckily, the quarterback overthrew him. It would've been six points if he hadn't. On the next play, the quarterback threw right back to him. It was a bunch right formation with two offensive linemen to block for him. "Screen! Screen! Help!" I yelled but no one paid attention to me. The ball was hiked and just like I read it, it was a screen. I laid out one of the linemen blocking for the wideout and tried to tackle him from behind but he dragged me for about five yards and my teammates helped me bring him to the ground.

After that game, I didn't want to play defensive back anymore. I felt out of my element. Being thrown into that fire was destroying my confidence. My defensive back coach said I had done OK for my first time in live action, but I felt I had played horribly. I didn't argue with him, though. I just worked to get better because it would help my team.

The next week, Coach Lute wanted us to go harder than usual. We were tackling on special teams, which we normally didn't do. On the first kickoff play, I ran down and made the tackle, but something was wrong. When I wrapped my arms around the returning receiver to bring him down, my right arm went dead. I couldn't feel my arm, so I pulled myself out. As I pulled back my shoulder pads, my arm started tingling.

"Bryant, what happened?" Coach Lute asked as he walked over to me. "When I made the tackle, it went dead," I said. "You all right?" he said. "Just shake it and wake it back up." I nodded in agreement but knew it wouldn't go away. "Man, forget that mess; this junk hurts," I said to myself. I knew something was wrong with my shoulder or arm. I sat out for the rest of practice that day. When I got home, it took three hours to do my homework. I couldn't lift my arm. I had to use my left hand to move my arm so I could write.

The next day I went to school early to get checked by our athletic trainer. "Mr. Tabb, I need you to check my arm," I said. "I think it's messed up pretty bad." He said, "Well, tell me what happened." "Yesterday, on kickoff," I said, "when I made the tackle on the returner, my whole arm went numb." "OK, let's check it out," he said, beginning to examine my shoulder joint. He began from the posterior side and worked his way anteriorly. Every few seconds he would ask if I felt any pain, which I did when he got to the anterior side of my humeral joint. "OK, Bryant, can you lift your arm?" he asked, holding my wrist for the resistance. I shook my head, "No, sir." "OK, can you hold your arm up?" he asked, this time holding my arm up. When he let it go, my arm fell right back down to my side. "Bryant, you have pretty bad injury," he said. "Your season is over. You need an MRI so we can see what exactly is wrong." I lowered my head as he confirmed what I had already assumed. The next step was to set up a meeting with the specialist to get a diagnosis and see how long I would be out.

The next week, I had an MRI performed. When I got in the machine, I closed my eyes for what seemed like 10 minutes before I was awakened by the controller of the machine. Next, we went to see the specialist so he could tell us what options we had. When he walked into the room my Mom and I shifted our focus on him, "Good morning," he said, "my name is Dr. Kellini." "Good morning, Doc," I said. "How are you?" "I'm doing well," he replied. "Thanks for asking. Well, let's get down to business, Bryant. I have some good news, and I have some bad news." While he was setting up the MRI pictures in the light, I replied, "Give me the bad news first, please." "The bad news," he said, "is your season is over. You have torn cartilage in the humeral joint socket." I sat there with a straight face to listen to how bad it was. "OK, now give me the good news, please, Doc. Hahaha," I said with a laugh to ease the sadness of not being able to play for the rest of the season. "Good news is," he said, "the tear is very minuscule and it is on the anterior edge of the humeral bone. Because it is so small, you can wait it out and see if it heals on its own or we can go in and scope it. Whatever you want to do; the choice is yours to make." I looked at my Mom, and said, "Mama, what do you think?" She just looked at me and shrugged her shoulders. We both laughed. I already knew what I wanted to do. "I want to wait and see if it heals on its own," I said. I looked at Dr. Kellini with a sure face. "OK," he said, "so I will set the next time I see you for February. That way, we will be able to find the next course of action." I smiled and said, "Thank you so much, Dr. Kellini." We said our good byes and we left.

The next morning, I told Mr. Tabb that I decided to let it heal on its own. He said he felt that was the best thing to do, because I was still young and growing and my body would heal itself. He gave me a band and a few arm and shoulder exercises to do. He told me to do them at least twice a day but no more than three times a day. He gave me a sling and told me to wear it for a few weeks. I really didn't want to wear it, but if Mr. Tabb said to do it, I did. I put the sling on before I left the training room. "Dang! I gotta wear this during school," I thought.

"Bryant, what's wrong? What did you do?" said Mrs. Gee when I walked into her math classroom. She was an awesome math teacher. She also was a Christian who oftentimes invited me to church. Her husband was a pastor, and they were in the process of planting a church. "I tore cartilage in my shoulder," I said. "I did it at practice, tackling someone." "I thought you played offense," she said. "Why are you tackling people?" "Well, Mrs. Gee," I said. "I play special teams as well, and during special teams you have to tackle." "Oh! OK," she said. "Well, I will be praying for your shoulder, and its healing." I smiled and nodded as the bell rang for class to start. I wondered why everyone always said she was hard and really mean. People told me to change my class, because she had too many rules. I stayed because rules didn't bother me. Over the course of the semester, she just showed kids she cared. She just made you care about yourself. I had promised her that when they found a building to have their church services in, I would come. The rest of the day, I told teachers, friends and teammates what had happened to my shoulder. I wanted to take that sling off so bad so everyone could stop asking me what had happened.

A FEW MONTHS LATER...

Finally, a few months later, I was able to go to school without my sling. My shoulder was strong enough that I could raise and lower it in a slow, controlled movement. The exercises Mr. Tabb gave me worked amazingly well and when the football team worked out in fourth block, I would do isometric exercises, core exercises and neck exercises, because I was not cleared to join them for regular weight lifting. I wanted to be as strong as possible when I got back to the team, though. I was so excited because I would get to see the specialist in a few days, and I knew I would be cleared because I was sure God would answer the prayers everyone and I had made about my being healed. It was only a matter of days now, and I would be able to go back to my normal life. I just stayed calm and kept working. On Thursday, my Mom checked me out of school to go see Dr. Kellini. I was excited, because I knew it was the day I would be cleared to play football again. When we got to the specialist's office, it was the same procedure as last time. I got in the machine, but this time I didn't go to sleep, I was too amped to sleep in there even though it felt like I was in the machine for about thirty minutes. After I got out of the machine, we were escorted into a room to wait for Doc to walk in. "Bryant, what's up bigin'?" Dr. Kellini said when he walked in about five minutes later. "How are you feeling?" I told him I was feeling great. "How are you? Give me the bad news first," I said. We both laughed. He said he was doing great. "It is good to see you smile like that," he said. "All right, the bad news is . . . I don't have any. All I have is good news for you. Good news is, you are cleared. Your body healed itself." I just smiled and looked at my mother and said, "I told you, Mama." Dr. Kellini said I was blessed because he had seen similar cases in other people who did not heal on their own. "Yes, sir," I said and just smiled and thanked God because I knew it was Him. "You are full go from here on out," Kellini said. "There will be soreness, and there might be a little pain, but that is from scar tissue build up. If you have any stiffness or excess pain, do not push it. Just work your way back in slowly and progressively." He told me not to show off and to save my energy for Friday nights in football season. "Yes, sir, Doc," I said.

"Now it is time to get back to school and share the great news with everyone," I thought as we shook hands with Dr. Kellini, thanked him once more and headed out to the car. "You wanna just come home?" Mom said. "No, ma'am," I said. "Today is Admiral ball. I will just ride home with Marques." Mom said, "OK," and when she took me back to school it was fourth block. I got out of the car, ran up to Coach Lute and gave him the paper from Doc that said I was cleared. "Well, what are you waiting for? Go get dressed," he said. I bolted into the locker room, changed into my football attire and came back out of the building headed straight to the field where everyone was. They had just started picking the teams, so it was perfect timing. When I got close enough for my teammates to hear me, I said, "So, who's gonna pick me up?" Everyone turned around and got excited to see me back and able to play with them. It felt great to be back with my boys. It was time to put the work in. When the teams were picked, my team had to start on defense first. I lined head up on my man, because we were in cover 1. When the ball was hiked, my guy ran a deep post. I lagged behind to bait the quarterback. I looked up and the ball was coming to my man. The logical movement would have been to throw my left hand in the air to bat the ball down, but this was one chance where I could test my right shoulder. I left my feet and used my right arm to bat the ball down. When my hand touched the ball, I forcefully pulled my arm down to throw the ball down. That movement did give me a little pain, but I knew I could do it. I just had to re-strengthen it. As I came back to the ground, I lost my footing and fell. Everyone paused to see if I was OK. I popped back up, jiggled my right arm to loosen it up more. "Bryant, you all right?" one of my teammates asked. "Yeah, bra. I'm good." I answered with a smile and dapped him up as I jogged back into position to get ready for the next play. "I'm back," I thought.

The next day I went to see Mrs. Gee to tell her that I had gotten cleared. "You know you promised me that you would come to Bible study," she said. "Yes, ma'am," I said. "I will go this Friday if Coach Carter lets me leave early." I worked in the concession stand for the basketball games. "OK," Mrs. Gee said. "I will see you Friday." I left and was headed to my next class for the day. I didn't even know who we were playing on Friday; I just knew we had a game. If we were playing a team that would bring a lot of fans I most likely would not be able to make it. Later that day in football, Coach Lute called everyone into the team room because he had an announcement to make. "We have been invited to Florida State University; they are allowing us to bring twelve players to spring practice to represent Gulfport High School. From here on out everyone will be getting tallied for everything. So be on time and come ready to work because the coaching staff will be choosing the twelve players to go watch a college practice."

I just knew I would be one of the twelve because I did everything I was supposed to do and more. There was no doubt in my mind that I would be going. I just had to do what I normally do. "Men," Coach Lute said, "we will be going to this spring practice the second weekend of our spring practice. As we get closer to that time we will give further instructions." As the Coach finished his sentence, I looked toward the back of the room and saw a few basketball players in our block. I was confused, because I knew those guys did not play football. I was curious as to why they were there. They should've been in the gym. "I would like all of you to welcome a few of your fellow athletes to the football team," Coach Lute said. "A few members from the basketball team have decided to come out and play. I think they will help us in our skill positions, give us the depth that we need and give us a shot to be great." After he said that all I could think was, "I hope they are ready for the hits they are about to receive, 'cause this ain't nothing like basketball." Coach dismissed us to go get dressed for weights and conditioning.

Friday came, and I passed Mrs. Gee in the hallway on the way to class. "Tonight at seven o'clock we are having Bible study," she said. "Where will you be?" "I will be here, at the gym working the concession stand," I answered. "OK, I will be at the gym to pick you up at six thirty," she said and I gave her a slight grin, "Yes, ma'am." I headed to class so I wouldn't be late. That day seemed to go by so fast. Next thing I knew, we were in fourth block for football, lifting weights and doing our conditioning work. Before I knew it, school was out and Dallas and I went to the gym because we had to work the basketball game. We got everything set up just the way Coach Carter liked it. When he walked in I asked, "Aye, Coach, can I leave early tonight?" He looked at me with a scrunched face and said, "Leave early? For what?" "Well," I said, "I promised Mrs. Gee that I would go to Bible study tonight." He said he wasn't sure about that and asked what time it started. "It starts at seven," I said adding that she would be coming to get me at six thirty. "Like I said, Bryant," he said, "we will have to see because that's usually the time when we are the busiest." I just nodded my head, because I knew that was really a no. He just didn't come right out and say it. I was going to try my luck, though, and see what he said when the time came for me to leave. Six thirty came so fast, I wasn't able to keep an eye on the clock because it was a double-header game, and we got busy in the concession stand. "Bryant! You ready?" I heard Mrs. Gee's voice from the window. I looked at Coach Carter and he shook his head. "Mrs. Gee, I can't go. I will go next week, I promise." "Boy, you are going to make me late for church," she said with a little giggle while she was running out of the gym to go to church.

The following week was the start of spring football, but I couldn't take part in it because I also ran track, and that week was the South State track meet. Unfortunately, I did not qualify at South State to go to the state track meet in the hurdles or pole vault. I was not an alternate for any other relays, so after South State, my track season was over, and I was free to go back to football. I also kept my promise to Mrs. Gee and went to Bible study. I knew I wanted to leave the church I was attending at the time and attend her church. Pastor Gee, her husband, presented the word of God in a way I had never experienced. I knew in my spirit he was the pastor I needed to be led by. When I told him my decision, he said I needed to wait before just leaving the church I was attending to join theirs. He told me to pray about it and wait a few weeks before finalizing my decision. I told him I would. I had already left my current church mentally, though. When you know, you know, and I knew that I was supposed to be with the Gees' church.

When I got back to football for spring, I saw that all the basketball players were starters or in the second-string spots. I was a bit confused because they hadn't experienced what it was like to be in pads. They had only been in shells the past week. All they were doing was thudding up and not being taken down to the ground. I wanted to know how many would last after we did our full-out scrimmage on Wednesday. I did not like that they were thrust into starting roles with no football experience. I really felt disrespected by Coach Lute from that move, but I did not have any control over that so I tried my best to help them with the plays. I also tried to teach them the routes. They actually looked really good in routes on air, but when it came to running some of the routes when the defense was out there, they were scared to get hit. On slants, digs, drives and whip routes, they were scared of getting hit. They would drop the ball. On hitches, outs, go's, and post routes, they caught the ball. They were decent athletes. They just needed some football toughness to be great at the football level.

During the scrimmage on Wednesday the defense was really taking it out on the basketball players. They were hitting them every chance they got. Part of it was because they were talking trash since the first week. I did think it was a bit funny because the basketball players were a bit confused about the rules. They didn't know they could get hit every play. One of them got hit so hard running a slant, he quit on the spot. That probably was the funniest thing I had seen in a long time. We saw Coach Lute try to stop him, "Where you going?" he said. "What are people going to think about you?" He looked at coach while shaking his head and said, "Coach, I'm going home. I don't care what anyone thinks about me. You get hit too much in this sport. I'm going back to basketball." Everyone on the practice field kind of stopped to watch what was happening. Coach Lute turned around and said, "Anybody else want to leave? Go now!" Everyone just looked at each other but didn't move. "All right, men, let's be great," Coach said. "We only need people that want to be out here with us." After that statement we went back to finish the scrimmage. At the end of practice Coach Lute said we would find out soon who was going to Florida State's practice on Saturday.

The next day at football, we were off because we had a really good first two weeks. We had a team meeting in fourth block because Coach had to tell us who was going on the trip the next day to watch FSU's practice. "OK, men," he said, "as you know, we told you that we would take twelve people to watch a real division one practice." I sat up in my chair because I knew he was going to be taking me on that trip. I worked too hard to come back from my injury not to get invited to be a part of that amazing experience. He didn't call my name, and I was a tad bit confused because he called the name of every basketball player who had just joined the team. He only called one football player's name. Everyone was OK with that football player going, but everyone was a bit shocked that he chose the basketball players over the true football players. In my mind, he picked the basketball players as an incentive to encourage them to stay on the team. I did not think they would stay on the team after the weekend. I really could not believe he was taking the basketball players. That was my introduction to the politics of the sports industry, and I made up my mind from that day on that I would always put myself in position for the politics to work in my favor. My plan for that to work was very simple: work harder than I already did, put myself in position to make every play I could, and make sure there was nothing the coach or coaches could say about why I shouldn't play.

The next week all the basketball players left the team, except for one, which is just about what I had thought would happen. They just stayed long enough to go to FSU's spring practice. At practice on Monday, the receivers were working on the goal-line fade ball. On my turn, I jumped up and caught the ball in the end zone, lost my footing and fell. "Bryant, come here," Coach Lute said. I jogged over to him, "Yes, sir?" I said. "Come on, now. You're better than that," he said. "I don't understand, Coach. What do you mean?" I said. "Keep your feet," he said. "When you catch the ball, stay on your feet." "Yes, sir," I said nonchalantly. "Bryant, you are the most athletic receiver on the team," he said. I stopped and looked at him with a face of disbelief. "He is only saying that because all the basketball players quit on him," I thought after I heard that last statement. "I'm serious, you are," he said. "Now when are you going to start showing it?" "I got you, Coach," I said. "All right," he said. "Let me see it." I nodded and jogged to get back in line with the rest of the receivers.

SUMMER OVERVIEW

That summer my work ethic tripled. I went to every scheduled weight-training and pass Skelly with the team on top of staying later to run more routes and catch the ball. On off days for the team, I was playing flag football with the old heads on the weekends.

If I was not involved with football, I was at church, helping out Pastor Gee or Lady Gee with anything I could. That summer it was church and football. I started to see production not only in football but also in my relationship with God. We went to a 7-on-7 camp in the month of June. That was the first test of the summer to see if all the work I had been putting in would help. My hard work paid off in perfect fashion. We played about eight games, and I was catching the ball in traffic, had more separation between the defender and myself, and I saw the most improvement from the work I had put in during the beginning of the summer.

My relationship with God grew tremendously as well. I was able to talk to Him without hesitation in prayer. I started reading the Bible on my own to get more of an understanding of how a Christian life is supposed to be lived. I saw things begin to change in me. I began wanting to go to church more and more. I loved going, felt guilty if I missed it. Pastor Gee always challenged the congregation to be better in every facet of life, as long as we were in God's will. He encouraged us to read books to enhance our relationships with God and also to enhance our relationships with one another. Everything that my pastor was giving I would use now or in the near future. He would always say, "If you don't need this word right now do not throw it out. Get this spiritual food in your spirit so that when you need to use this word it will be available. It is better to have and not need, than to need and not have." So, I took that and gained as much information about God as I could handle at that age.

The last camp before the end of the summer was at The University of Southern Mississippi. I discovered that I had the confidence as a player that I had lacked the previous fall. I walked with a little bit of savvy and moxie that day. I was confident in the work I had put into my craft. That made me play very loose and in rhythm. The timing the quarterback and I had was amazing; no matter where he put the ball, if it was in my vicinity, I caught it. That was the day I showed Coach Lute that I was a "player," as he would say. I saw everything that I had been working for show up at that camp. Now, I just had to maintain it through the fall.

After the camp I went home, took a shower and walked into the living room to see what my mother was doing. "Mama, what are you watching?" "My cooking shows," she answered fixing her eyes on me. "How was the camp?" "It was great. We went four and one." "How did you do? Did you score any touchdowns?" "Yeah," I said, "I had about five of them. All the receivers were scoring, honestly. We looked really good, Mama." She smiled and gave me a high five, "Get ready for this year, Mama, because I am going to blow up," I said with pure confidence. I knew that year was going to be an amazing year for me. She just smiled, and said, "OK." "Mama," I said, "I'm serious." "OK, Bryant," she said. She did not believe but that was OK because I did. The only thing I had to do was show her.

"As a man thinketh, so is he." -- *Proverbs 23:7*

Time to process/recondition your thoughts
Questions

1. What unexpected things occurred in your life?
2. Have you kept pushing?
3. Why or Why not?

CHAPTER 4

Flash of The promise:
Some See and Still Don't Believe

JUNIOR YEAR

Fall camp was here, and I was ready. All the work I had put in during the summer gave me confidence that I would make some noise at the receiver position. The first game was against Northeast Jones High School. It was a strange game, because we were having quarterback trouble. Nobody was sure who our guy would be until the starter came back from an injury. So, we were forced to use a young quarterback, which was fine until he and Coach got into it during halftime and he got kicked off the team. Coach put Damien at quarterback. His first position was receiver. He could throw the ball decently, though, and we had been practicing with him at the quarterback spot just in case we needed to go there for an emergency. Well, it was an emergency because Northeast Jones was beating us badly. Nothing had been going our way that night. We went three and out pretty much all of our possessions. The second possession in the third quarter, we showed signs of a little life. We started with the ball on the fifteen-yard line. Set up with bad field position because of a bad return, Dallas got a zone read and turned that into first down. That was one of the few positive plays we had. Coach Lute called a timeout, "OK, men, here we go," he said. "Let's go get some points now. Damien, what do you want to call? Do you want another run or are you ready to throw?" "Yeah, Coach. Let me throw it. We are going for the money. All go's," he said with excitement. "OK, go make it happen," Coach Lute replied. Damien looked at me, "All right, B. You ready? 'Cause I'm coming to you." I nodded my head. I was ready to make a play. Our timeout ended, and we jogged back on to the field. I felt adrenaline pumping through my body. "You have to make this play for your team," I thought. We lined up in two-by-two; I'm in the slot position on the right side. Damien hiked the ball. I took off, dipped and ripped through the linebacker, turned and looked for the ball. There it was in the air. He had thrown a perfect pass, and I plucked it out of the air. I took off running toward the end zone. I could hear our sideline erupt, and it gave me more energy to hold my top-end speed. As I got close to the end zone, the defenders hit my foot, and I started high-stepping. Then I felt someone jump on my back, and he wrestled me down at the three yard line. We lined up real fast, ran a zone read, and Dallas scored. We were finally on the board. After that drive, nothing else went right for us. We lost that game 49-7.

We got our starting quarterback back for the next game, and we knew we would be a force offensively. We were a fast-paced offense already, and now that we had our main man at the helm, we would go even faster. We could now call two and three plays at a time and not miss a beat. Whether it was a positive play or not, we were going to roll with it. Coach Lute made sure we were in shape by making us run sprints for loafs, turnovers and missed assignments. His goal for us was to be efficient and fast. That week's practice was hard, because for every turnover or missed assignment we had in last week's game, we ran. That week we were headed to Hattiesburg to play the Tigers. Coach said we would open the playbook up a little bit since we had everyone back in their spots now. The first play of the game would be all hitches or sliver key. Sliver key was the name of a screen Coach had put in for me. The first play of the game was all hitches opened up with something simple. The next play was silver key. When the ball was snapped, I took two baby steps up and one big step back to catch the ball. It made one guy miss to the inside. I looked up field and saw my teammates set their blocks up perfect. I went back to the outside, and I was gone. I ran for a fifty-six yard touchdown. As I got back to the sideline Coach said, "Bryant, you ready?" "Coach, can you get someone else to run this time for me?" The special teams coach looked at me with a crazy face and said, "One play? You can't go one more play?" "Yeah, Coach," I conceded, and the coach thanked me. I just needed the time to catch my second wind. Then I would be good. The assistant special teams coach came to me and said, "I know you are a little winded. I know you just caught a pass and ran for a fifty-six-yard touchdown, but your team needs you on the field every chance possible. Big players make big plays in big games, and, young man, you are a big player." I smiled and nodded to Coach and got into my spot. That game was really a track meet because both offenses scored so quickly. We lost that game 61-49. We stalled out in the first half on two drives and that came back to haunt us at the end of the game. I finished the game with nine receptions for 109 yards and three touchdowns.

Next up was the Petal Panthers. We came out of the gate firing on all cylinders. We jumped out on them quick. It was finally coming together. We looked up, and it was 20-0. Coach Lute called a time out. "Men, I say we go for two right here and put the nail in the coffin right before halftime." Coach Lute was far from being an ordinary coach. He would call off-the-wall stuff, and most of the time we had his back. This was not one of those times. "No, Coach. Just kick the field goal," I said. "Yeah, Coach. We are already up three touchdowns," Damien said. "Are y'all saying that you don't believe in your teammates?" Coach Lute said. This was not the time to argue or explain why we disagreed with what he was about to call. So, I just shook my head, "I believe in my teammates, Coach." "All right, then," he said. "Let's go for it and kill them right here."

It was the big boy package that we had been working on that week. We did not convert. We ended the half with twenty points instead of twenty-one. Everyone was kind of mad at Coach for making that call. It killed our momentum. In the second half, Petal would rally thirty-five unanswered points and beat us 35-20. That was probably my worst game because I had a lost fumble, and they scored off my turnover. I felt so bad; the eight receptions for one hundred six yards and a touchdown meant nothing to me because I had lost the ball.

The next two losses we had hurt the worst, because they came to our longtime rivals Harrison Central and Biloxi. Harrison Central is in the north part of Gulfport, and we had been on a streak of beating them for sixteen years. They just outright beat us. They made more plays than we did. They thoroughly gave us a good, old-fashioned butt-whooping. When the final buzzer went off and they stormed the field, it just crushed me. I felt so bad for the seniors of the team who went out losing to the Red Rebels. They will be the class forever known as the class who lost the streak. The last game of the regular season was against our neighboring city, the Biloxi Indians. This rivalry has been going on forever. We have been going back and forth in the series. We knew it would be a close game. We lost on the last play of the game. We ran all go's, and when the quarterback threw the ball, I thought he was throwing it to me, but it was going to my teammate who did not play much. He was open, though. I was bracketed in by defenders. I watched as the ball went in his direction. The defensive back left me and went over to defend the pass. I would normally go over to make sure my teammates caught the ball, but there were too many defenders. I decided to keep them with me, so it would be one-on-one. They both jumped up for the ball, and the Indians' defensive back took the ball out of my teammate's hand. Game over. We lost by four points.

That season was good and bad for me. Individually, I had a great season. I finished with forty-nine receptions for six hundred ninety-two yards and seven touchdowns. It was bad because I am a team-player, and I wanted the team's success to outweigh my individual success. We could not win. We always seemed to be one or two plays away from winning the game. Those one or two plays would have turned our season from 1-9 to 7-2. It didn't end up that way, though. That was the hardest season I had ever been through. As a leader on the team, what could you do to keep your team fighting even though the results came out the same? The whole season I kept asking myself, "What more can I do for my team to come out with a win?" On top of all that, I sensed Coach Lute might be out as the head coach soon. That was a bit tough for all the seniors, because we had been with him two years already and he knew us. We had grown with him. The new coach coming in really would not care about us. He would focus on his sophomore players because he would have them longer. We just had to get used to it, though. In the coaching profession, that is just the way the cookie crumbles. You either win or go home.

We soon found out that Coach Lute got a job with East Mississippi Community College. He came back to the school one day and asked to speak with me. "What's up, Coach Lute? How are you? Congratulations on getting on with East Mississippi," I said. He thanked me for the well-wishes and said things were going well for him. "Did you know this year that the state of Mississippi is opening up?" he said. "Opening up?" I said. "What do you mean?" I had a confused look on my face. "Well, there used to be regions that Junior Colleges could lock down and target players. All the players that were targeted in that JUCO's region — no other JUCOs could talk to. With you having the type of season you just had, you have raised interest in a few JUCOs, but no one could talk to you until now, because Mississippi Gulf Coast Community college (Perk) marked you as a target." I told him I understood what he was saying. "Great," he said, "so I'm coming to you first before anyone else does to let you know we want you. We want you to come be a Lion." "Really?" I said with a huge smile on my face. "Bryant, I'm serious as a heart attack," he said. "I have already talked to the head coach and showed him your film. He is onboard. Bryant, I know you. You are a playmaker; there is not another coach who knows you better than me. Come be a Lion and get you a ring, and then we will send you off to a big University where you can display your talent." That was when I got my first official offer to play at the next level. I didn't really have much to say, because I was taking it all in. "I know this is something that came at you a bit fast and may be a lot for you to take in at the moment," he said. "There is no rush. I just wanted you to know that we want you, because we know what you can do. I will be in touch with you soon." "OK, Coach," I said. "Thank you for the offer." "No problem, buddy," he said. "You earned it. You be good now, and I will come back and holler at you soon." We shook hands, and I went back to class. Coach left to go do some more recruiting. Honestly, I did not even have my eyes on going to junior college. I had made up my mind when I was eight years old that I would go straight to a university to play football. I was on track to do just that. All I had to do was have another season like the one I had just had, and I would reach the goal I had set for myself years ago.

NEW COACH

We didn't find out who our new head coach would be until the beginning of the spring semester. Everyone around the city couldn't stop talking about this guy. "He is an old-school coach. He will be in the Mississippi high school coaching hall of fame. He is going to get Gulfport back on track." That is all I was hearing around the city. Coach Don Banks was his name. He had coached at Madison Central, had four state titles and had a few players in the NFL. He had had a successful career. I saw him walking in the cafeteria after we got back to school from the Christmas holiday and introduced myself. "Hey,

Coach," I said. "I'm Bryant Lavender. I play receiver." "Hey, Bryant," he said. "I know who you are. I have watched film on you. Good player." "Thank you, coach," I replied. "You ready to make some plays this year?" he said. "I planned to throw to you forty to fifty balls this fall. We need you to make plays because that is what you do. You are a playmaker." "Yes, sir! I'm ready," I said. "Good," he said. "See you in the spring. Oh, wait. Do you run track?" "Yes, sir. I do," I said. He smiled and said, "Well, I will see you after you get done with that." Then he walked away, but he surprised me with how many balls he said he would throw me. Coming off a forty-nine reception, six hundred ninety-two yard and seven touchdown season was great. If he was going to stay true to his word then I knew this coming season would be better than the last individually for me. I was amped for spring, because it was the start of my senior campaign and my last chance to push for interest from the college scouts. I hoped Coach Banks was being honest with me and not just telling me what I wanted to hear. "Only time will tell," I thought, "but until then it was time to get ready for track season."

JUNIOR TRACK SEASON

As Dallas and I were getting ready for track practice, I asked, "Hey, bra, have you gotten any of those recruiting letters from colleges?" He looked at me with a nonchalant face and said, "Junk mail? Yeah, I have a whole bunch of them." I scrunched up my face as he said those words, "Are you going to keep them?" I asked. "No! Why would I keep junk mail?" he said. I was confused because I didn't see them as junk mail. I saw them as memories. "Well, I am going to keep mine," I said as we headed out to the track for practice.

After practice, I went home and looked at all the letters I had received. They were in my laundry cubby. There were letters from MSU, Ole Miss, Yale, Harvard, Princeton, Navy and Army, etc. I could see why Dallas called them junk mail, because they really didn't say much other than, "Bryant, we have you on our recruiting board. Keep up the good work." To me it was still cool to get the letters. Bank told me before he left, "B, the letters don't mean anything if they are not handwritten. That is how you know the coaches really want you." That made me go on the website called Scout.com. I would mainly go on that website to see the standings of teams in our region and how the tiebreaker worked if two teams were tied for a playoff spot, or just to be amused by the trash talk people engaged in about what teams were better than the others. That night the question, "Which players on the Coast are the best from Moss Point to Bay St. Louis?" I saw names written down, so I threw my name into the mix. "Bryant! Come here," my Mom was calling to me. "Yes, Ma'am," I logged off the computer and went to see what she needed. I did not check the website again until the next day after track practice. As I read the forum, it was cool to see the debates and opinions about different players. I saw Dallas' and Tommy's names on the list. Tommy went to D'Iberville. We played middle school and ninth-grade ball together. He moved after Hurricane Katrina hit. I was happy my two friends made the list of the best players on the Coast. Next, I saw a few people had replied to the entry of my name. Some comments were good and some were bad, but one of the worst ones stuck out to me.

"Bryant Lavender is a good player on a very bad team. Gulfport was horrible this year, so there is no telling if he is D1 caliber. If he transferred to Moss Point, Harrison Central, or Biloxi he would sit on the bench. He would see no playing time at all. I'm not even sure he could break the starting line up at Bay High. He is a 3rd stringer at best. He would not make Perk's squad let alone get a scholarship to a Division 1 school against top tier talent. I'm not bashing the kid, because I don't know him personally. I don't know how his grades are in school or if he gets in any trouble. But him playing football past high school, I don't see it. I just don't think he is good enough. I'm sorry."

I read that comment over and over. I wrote it down on a piece of paper and I put it in the back of my binder so I could read it every day. I used it as motivation. I knew in my heart I was good enough. In A&P class, I showed my friend Bernard what the person said and my teacher saw it while I was doing an assignment. She snatched it out and said, "Why do you have this in your binder? I'm getting rid of it!" She ripped it up into confetti and threw it into the trash. "Mrs. Little, why did you do that?" I said. "I was using that for motivation." "No!" she said. "That is not motivation, that is just pure negativity." "I am using it as fuel to make me go harder," I said. "That is stupid," she replied, giving me the meanest look I have ever seen her give. "Well, you asked, so I told you," I said and turned around and returned to my seat to pack my things before the bell rang. It didn't matter, because I made copies, so I could have more at home. She was so mad at me, but I really did use all the negativity people said about me and changed it into positive fuel to do even better in whatever they said I couldn't do.

That day at track practice everyone started asking Dallas and me if we were getting any letters or offers from schools. We both answered in unison, "A few." Coach Hood interjected, "Have y'all thought about going for track?" We laughed and answered in unison once more, "Naw!" followed with more giggles. "Why not? Both of you are good enough," she said. "I am going to be a regular student in college. I'm done taking part in sports after high school," Dallas said in answer to her question. "Dallas, stop telling that story," Coach Hood replied. "Aye, Coach," he said. "I hate track. I am only doing this to get faster, stay in shape and because my friends are running. I couldn't do this all year long." She looked at both of us with a "whatever" face. "Dallas, I'm not even going to listen to you," she said. "Your Daddy is not going to let that happen. And, Bryant, what if you don't get a scholarship to play football?" I cut her off immediately and said, "I am going to get one. Don't worry about it." "All I am saying," she said, "is not to count track out. I mean, it is not like the football team did good this year. Track can pay for school, too."

While she was saying that I was shaking my head the whole time. "Bryant, be real with yourself. You all went 1-9 this fall. What school is coming to see that?" I stared at her with a bit of anger in my eyes and said, "I am getting a scholarship." "All right, boss, whatever you say," she said. I couldn't believe what I had heard from one of my track coaches. I didn't care what she said, I was getting a scholarship.

Later that week I received an invitation to go to the Scout/Under Armor combine for high school athletes. I called Coach Coe to tell him the good news. "Coach, I got invited to the Scout/Under Armor combine. Do you know anything about it?" "Well," he said, "I believe you get evaluated by scouts and they send your number to college coaches." I got excited, and before I could ask my next question he said, "Do you know where they have you invited to?" I looked down at the paper, "Umm. It says New Orleans." "Oh, really," he said. "That means they will probably hold it in the Saints practice facility." "Really?" I said. "Yes," he replied. "That is where they hold those types of things. Are you going to go?" "I don't know, Coach," I said. "I have to ask my Mom if she can take me." "All right," he said, "call me back when you find out. That would be great publicity for you. You need to be there." "Yes, sir!" I hung up the phone with excitement for the possibility of being able to display my talent with some of the best athletes in my region. My Mom walked in from work, and when I saw her face, I could tell it had been a long day for her. I waited for her to relax and change clothes. "Mama," I said as I walked into the den. "I got invited to this combine in New Orleans." I handed her the printed-out invitation. As she read it, I tried to decipher her thoughts. "OK, Bryant, that's good," she said with a grin on her face. "Can you take me? It is this weekend." "I don't know," she said, "because I need tires for the van and the brakes are starting to go out. Did anyone else get invited to this combine?" "Yes, ma'am. Dallas did, but he told me he was not going." "Well," she said, "did you ask one of your coaches?" "Coach Coe knows about it," I said, "because I told him. But I don't know if he can take me. He may have something to do." "I'm sorry, baby," Mom said. "We are going to have to pass on this one." "Man! Mama, please!" My mother shook her head; I left the room disappointed, because I was afraid I would miss that opportunity. I went into my room and called Coach Coe back, "Coach, my Mom said she will not be able to take me." I heard Coach take a deep breath. "What time does it start?" he said. "It says 9 a.m." "OK, I'm going to clear my schedule tomorrow and take you." I could not believe he had just said that. "Thank you, Coach!" I said with a smile on my face. "'Thanks, Coach', nothing," he said. "You better not embarrass me over there." I chuckled and said, "No, sir!" He asked if I had all my gear. "Yes, sir," I said. "OK, I will pick you up at 7:15 a.m.," he said. "Make sure you carry your butt to sleep and get up in time to eat a decent breakfast." "Yes, sir." That night I made sure I put everything in my book bag, and I went to sleep early just as Coach had said to.

When my alarm went off, I got up, brushed my teeth, put my tights on and double-checked my bag to make sure I had all of my gear. I put my bag by the front door and went into the kitchen to fix a bowl of cereal. I already felt the butterflies in my stomach. "Morning, B," my Mom said as she walked into the kitchen to get some orange juice. "Morning, Mama." "Do you know how long the combine is?" she said. "No, I don't know, Mama. It just says it starts at 9 a.m." "OK, call me when you make it there and when you are on your way back." I nodded my head as I finished the last bit of my cereal. I put my bowl in the sink, picked up my book bag by the front door and walked outside to smell the morning air. As it turned 7:15 a.m., I saw Coach Coe pull up. I ran to the front door, "Mama, I'm gone." "OK, good luck!" she yelled back as she walked to the door to see me off. Before I knew it, we had traveled down Cowan/Lorraine and turned onto I-10 west, heading toward New Orleans. That was my first time riding with Coach, and I was a bit nervous. I was quiet for most of the trip because I did not know what to talk about. I just listened to the sports radio station he had playing on his radio. He broke the silence, "Do you have all your gear?" "Yes, sir." "Did you get enough to eat?" "Yes, sir." His voice was so deep that even when he was just asking regular questions it sounded like he was getting on to you. After that, we were quiet as mice. Occasionally I would glance over at him to see his facial expression. I just saw that he had a blank face, but at the same time he appeared to be deep in thought. I wasn't sure what he was thinking, but it made me think, "I gotta show out. And why did he do this for me? I didn't know he liked me this much." My thoughts ceased when his voiced sliced through the silence of the car ride. "You know why I brought you here, right?" When he said that I couldn't believe he knew what I was thinking. I didn't answer because I really wasn't sure why he brought me. "Brought you here," he said, "because, One: I believe in you. Two: You need the exposure." I just stared at him, because I did not have anything to say to that. We pulled into the parking lot, "Now, when you get in this building, you perform like I know you can, like you have been coached to perform. At these types of things, you need to get as many reps as possible. Don't be afraid to be first. Just know how to do the drill if you go first. Lastly, sell out. Go after every ball. If it is in your zip code, you come down with it." "Yes, sir," was all I had for him after he had given me that last bit of information.

We parked the car, got out, and I looked up and saw hundreds of kids going to the same place I was. Never having been to anything like that, I kept my head on a swivel to soak up the moment. We went in and found the registration table to check in. I was instructed to go into the weight room to get my height and weight checked. When I got to the room a man was there, "Good morning, Big Time! Take that off, and put this on. We dressin' y'all in Under Armor today." I immediately heard his New Orleans accent. He handed me a shirt and shorts. I put my shorts on and as I am putting on my shirt he asked me, "Where you from, Big Time?" I put my arms through my shirt and said, "Gulfport, Mississippi."

"Oh, you just down the street. What position do you play?" "Receiver." "Oh, you a big-time receiver, yeeeaaah." I stepped down off the scale, and he told me to go to the Under Armor representative to choose between gloves or cleats. Of course, I choose gloves because as a wideout you can never have too many gloves. Then I made my way to the field to warm up and meet some other athletes. I got Coach Coe to throw me a few balls to warm up my hands. "Why don't you just go find a quarterback that is participating in the combine with you," Coach said, "that way you have some type of chemistry. If you get a chance to hook up with him, you both will be comfortable with one another." "OK," I said.

As I began to scan the room for a quarterback, I saw a majority of them were already throwing to receivers. "Hey, there is a quarterback from the Coast over there. Come on, let's go see if he doesn't mind throwing it to you," said Coach Coe after he had spotted a kid from St. Stanislaus. As we walked up, we introduced ourselves. I shook hands with the quarterback and said, "It's good to see another Mississippi player. I'm Bryant." "What's up, man? I'm Jake." "Can I catch the ball for you?" "Sure thing, boss," he said and fired the ball to me. I grinned because he had some umph on it. He paused and said, "Give me a target with your hands. Don't move other than rotating with me." I nodded in understanding with him. I put my hands at chest level. He fired about ten balls at my chest as we rotated together in a circle. I didn't have to move my hands. Perfect balls. All I had to do was catch, squeeze and tuck.

Whistles sounded. "Showtime," I thought as I jogged to get in line to start the combine with a full team warm-up. We were given stickers to wear with numbers on them. We were told to keep the numbers visible at all times, because that was how they knew who we were. After the warm-up, they broke us up by positions. We started with the base testing, which was a forty-yard dash, a broad-jump, an L-drill, a vertical jump and the pro-shuttle. When we started the testing drills every now and again I would scan the building just to get a look at everything. The place was alive with whistles, yelling and different noises coming from the athletes. It felt good to be there with all the competition in one place. We only got two attempts at each drill, so I gave my best at all of them. When we were at the vertical jump test, our last drill before we went into individual drills, it got to be my turn. "Next," said the worker for that drill. I stepped up and he said, "What's your number?" "Eight," I answered. "OK, put your arm up." I raised my right arm up, and they raised it up until the blue line was even with my middle finger. Locked it in place, "OK, it's on you. Jump when you ready." After I heard those words, I looked up to the plastic bars sticking there. I picked a target to reach for, looked down at my feet and elevated. "Ttttkkkkk," was the sound when I hit the plastic bars. The man working my side of the vert test looked with a confused face at me, as if he couldn't believe what I had just done. I turned my head and looked at the measuring contraption to see what it was reading. It read 35 inches. "OK, on you," the man said again. I reset my feet and elevated again, this time producing more force so I could jump higher. "Tttkkk," the same noise came but this time not as loud. Landing in a three-point stance, I caught myself from falling, and again the man looked at me with a stunned face. He called another worker over and whispered in his ear. The other worker looked at me with a smile, and a few other athletes congratulated me on my good jump. That time I had gotten 37 inches.

I saw a guy who was wearing a white-collared shirt, khaki pants and carrying a clipboard. He was walking around writing notes down. He walked up to the guy working our vert test. They talked for a little bit, and I saw the worker point at me. The clipboard guy walked over to me and said, "Young man, what is your number?" "Eight," I answered. After everyone finished the drills, they gave us a ten-minute water break. I ran over to Coach Coe and he said, "How do you feel?" "I feel great," I said. "Did you see me on the drills?" "Yeah, I saw you," he said. "You looked good. Stay focused." "Yes, sir." "You need to get over to where you are supposed to be and be ready to go." I handed him my drink, got my gloves out of my bag and jogged over to where the wideouts were meeting for our individual drills. As I sat on the sideline to stretch my back, this other wideout walked up, "What up, bra? I'm Ty. How are you?" I stood up and said, "What up?" and shook his hand. "I'm, Bryant. I'm good, bra, how are you?" "Shoot, man," he said, "I'm good as well. How do you think you did on the testing?" "I feel I did all right," I said, "like I held my own." "Me, too," he said, "I'm just ready to start our position drills, one-on-ones, and seven-on-seven." "We get to do all that?" I said. "Yep," he said, "that way we can ball on these dudes." I laughed and replied with, "You know it." They blew the whistle for us to start our Indy drills, and I looked at my new friend, "Aye, Ty, where you from?" "I'm from Texas," he said. "What about you, B?" "I'm from Mississippi," I said as we got in our spots for the stick drill with one-hand catches at the end. Our position coach for the combine was real cool but started getting mad because everyone was rushing through trying to show their speed. "Stop! Everyone, listen up!" he said. "This drill is emphasizing the stick, so be relaxed about it. Go slow and be precise." "B," Ty said, "you know how to do this drill?" "Yeah," I said, "all you are doing is jogging and sticking. We do this all the time at practice." "Cool," he said, "I'm going to watch you and do it just like you." I nodded as I watched the other receivers go. They either looked uncoordinated or were going too fast. I wanted to be the first person to get it right out of the group. As I started the drill, I began in a jog, one □ two □ stick □. one □ two □ stick □ one □ two □ stick. Our position coach yelled, "Yeah! Y'all see that? That's how you do that! Let me see your swag." I did my last stick, and he released the ball for me to go get it. I snagged it with my left hand. After I jogged back to the group, the clipboard guy came up to me, "What is your number?" "Eight," I replied. He chuckled a little bit and said, "I've already come to you." I just smiled and focused back on the drill we were doing for my turn to go again. When it was my turn to go again the coach had a little smile on his face. This time he stood in front of me, and every time I stuck he bobbed his head like my feet were hitting a drum. After that it was time to go to one-on-ones versus the defensive backs.

I looked at Ty and said, "It's time to ball." He smiled and said, "Yes, sir." That part of the combine was a little tricky because it was what everyone had been waiting on. There were hundreds of kids trying to do the same thing I was doing -- get seen and recognized for their ability to play this wonderful game of football. On my first rep I wanted to go short and run a slant route. The defensive back was playing off-man technique. I lined up, looked inside and waited on the movement of the ball. Hut! One, two and three stick on my third step. The quarterback threw a perfect ball. I caught it, burst upfield and jogged back to get in line. It was seven minutes before I got another chance to go again. That time, I chose to run a ten yard out as I lined up on the line and looked at the defensive back. He was in cover three technique, seven yards off and a yard inside. Hut! I exploded off the ball, and I kept him to my inside because I would beat him easily just off of body position. At the top of my route I gave a good stick and the defensive back froze. I broke out toward the sideline and turned to track the ball. The ball came out high; I jumped up, made the catch and dragged my toe on the way down. I jogged back to the line and saw that Jake was the fourth one in line. I wanted to go with him, so I stared at him until we made eye contact. He mouthed the word, "Post." I smiled and nodded to the route he gave me. "Hey, you guys, get in a line," we heard the coaches say. When that happened, I got pushed back about three people. Jake saw what happened so he dropped behind two people and then he pretended to tie his shoe and winked at me. When he stood up and got in line we were back together. When it was our turn I lined up on the line, and I noticed the defensive back was pressing. I didn't want to get jammed, so I planned out my release and looked inside at the ball. I locked eyes with Jake right before he hiked the ball and he smiled at me. Hut! I worked my out-in-out release, hit his forearm then chopped his hand down. I got off the line and I put the burners on him. I stuck at the top of my route and looked for the ball. I had to put it in another gear, because Jake had let it go. "Concentrate. Concentrate," I thought, as I focused in on the ball. Here it is, arms up, and I came down with it. When I turned around I saw a few people clapping. I saw Jake jogging toward me. He gave me a dap and said, "Great catch, Bryant." I replied, "Shoot! Great throw!" After that, we had a water break before we were going to pass skeleton. I scanned the place to see where Coach Coe was, and I saw that he had started helping out the people who were running the camp.

I hoped Jake and Ty would be on my team for the last period of the day. When they chose the teams, we got separated. I called out the x-receiver in my group; we would start in empty left formation. The play was stick concept. I had a slant backside. When we took the field to run our play, I looked at my side of the defense. "Hut!" I ran my slant expecting the ball because I was open, but the quarterback threw it to the out route. I jogged back to the huddle and Coach Coe said, "Tell the QB to throw it to you." I replied, "I can't do that." I got into the huddle. For the next play we were running the simple smash concept. The quarterback sent the running back on a streak up the middle. We got to the line for my team's second rep. "Hut!" He threw the corner route on my side, but it was incomplete; the defense covered it. The safety batted the ball to the ground. When I jogged back to the huddle, I caught Coach Coe's face and I knew what that look was for. This was to be the last play, and we had all goes. There would be a few minutes before we went up. I slid over to the quarterback and said, "Look my way, bra. I got you." He nodded to my statement. I went over to stand by the area of the field where I would be while I waited on our turn to go. I glanced over at the quarterback as we were about to take the field. I saw Coach Coe pointing in my direction. I guessed he was giving him an extra push to throw it in my direction. I took the line and looked at the ball for its movement. "Hut!" I came off the ball and ran right past the defensive back who was covering me. The quarterback let it fly in my direction. The ball was a tear drop; the safety ran over as the ball came down out of the air. He jumped to swat the ball down but missed, and I caught it right behind him. Touchdown! My squad ran over to me, and we celebrated as a team. I looked over to Coach Coe with a smile, and he just nodded his head. "I just killed it," I thought.

At the end of camp, we had a few people give closing remarks to the whole group. Ty and I linked back up right before it was time to go. They had food for us in the cafeteria and after we finished eating, the combine would be officially over. Ty and I found a table to eat at, and we sat down and started shooting the breeze, talking about different things. The clipboard guy came and sat down next to us. He asked where we were from, what high schools we went to, and what our grade levels were in school. He thanked us for talking to him; he got up and went off to another table. "All right, Bryant, I am about to get out of here, man. We have a long drive back to Texas. It was nice to meet you, bra," Ty said. "All right, bra," I said. "As soon as I find where my Coach is we are going to get on this road as well. It was nice to meet you, homie." We got up from the table, threw our trash away, dapped each other up and went our separate ways. I found Coach Coe. He was finished up with his network talk and then we went to the car to head home. I was waiting for Coach to tell me how I did, but he didn't start with that. "Who was that guy in the collar shirt and khakis?" he asked. "I don't know," I said. "He was walking around all day asking people for their number. I think he was a reporter." "Oh, OK," Coach said. "He came up to Ty and me at the end," I said, "to ask us a few questions about where we were from, and what schools we went to. Coach, how did I do?" He turned to look me in the eye and said, "You did what you were coached to do." I was kind of waiting for a smile, but he kept a straight face. "What did you say to the QB in my group?" I asked. "I just told him that you were the best wideout there," he said, "that if he put it in your zip code you would come down with it." I just smiled. I didn't know he thought I was that good. For the rest of the ride I was in and out of sleep. When I got home I took a shower and went back to sleep.

Back at school we were finishing up the track season. We had the South State meet coming up, so I knew practice would be a bit hard. Everyone knew I had gone to that combine over the weekend so they asked me about it and how I did. I told them I did well, and I would find out if I made the all combine team probably by the end of that week. I later went home and checked the Scout.com website to see if anything had been posted about the combine that had taken place the past weekend. There was an article titled Lavender Breaks out in the Big Easy. It explained my excitement for the opportunity to be able to attend the combine, that I had done well against some of the top talent at the camp and that I had made a strong push to be selected for the all-combine team. Just then, I had a praise break in the computer room, and I thanked God for allowing me to perform as well as I did.

Most of the upperclassmen track members hung out with each other because our first sport was out of season. When fourth block came, we either practiced or we waited until after school to run. If I waited until after school, the majority of the time, I would be talking to Coach Pee. There were a few of us talking to her when Coach Carter said, "Bryant, come here. I want to show you something." I went to his office. I had no idea what for and said, "What's up, Coach?" "How are you feeling about the meet this weekend?" he said. "Straight," I said. "It is just like any other meet. I just have to do what I do. Is there something that I should be worried about?" "No," he said. "You know that kid from Meridian has the fastest time in the high hurdles and in the 300s." I knew exactly who he was talking about. That guy was a beast in the hurdles. I didn't have anything on him. "Yeah, Coach. I know," I said in answer to him. "Did you see the times he put up at the north regional meet?" he said. "No, sir," I said. He looked at me with a grin and said, "Thirteen five." I just busted out laughing and said, "Oh, yeah, buddy. Runnin'!" He showed me the time sheet for both races and both times were so fast. "Coach, everyone is running fast times, what is up with that?" I asked because nobody down in the south region had times like the ones up north. "Are they doing something we don't?" Coach just chuckled and said, "No, you just don't have any other competition on there than the kid from Biloxi. You will be fine when they come down here. I just wanted to show you that you are going to have to run." "I do run, Coach," I said. "What are you trying to say?" He got a serious look and said, "I am saying that you need to run the whole race for the 300 hurdles." I know why he said that because I thoroughly disliked running that race. I would just stride the race normally and only sprint when someone was close to me. Coach Carter threw the time sheet on his desk, and I looked down to see the 300 hurdle times and saw 37, 38 and 39 on the sheet. I just shook my head and walked out. "You know what you have to do," he yelled as I walked out to change for practice. I knew that day's practice was going to be tough. I had two four hundreds and two starts for my three hundred hurdles. I had to work on my high hurdles, and I had to break in a new pole for pole vaulting. I was a bit scared with my new pole because the top height on it said 13 feet, 9 inches. I had been winning every pole vault that year with a meager 11 feet, 6 inches, because no one in our district or region had a solid vaulter. That meet, I would have to at least jump 12 feet to secure a spot to go to state in that event. The week flew by, and before I knew it, Saturday had arrived.

My goal for that meet was to make it to state. Field events started first, and pole vault was one of the first to begin. About ten minutes after I started jumping, the high hurdles would take place and right after that, the two-mile run. When I checked in at pole vault, I told them I was about to run the hurdles, and they said I just needed to give them a height start for pole vault. I am going to come in at 10 feet, 6 inches. I went to check in for the hurdles, and I started to get butterflies in my stomach. I saw the Meridian kid, and I knew if I stayed closed to him that I would be just fine. I found out that I was in lane two, which is not a good lane. Coach Pee looked at me, smiled and said, "You ready, lil' boy?" I chuckled and said, "Yeah, Coach. I'm ready." "All right, run fast," she said, walking to the finish line to get the time and see the finish. Everyone started setting up their blocks and some people did a few warmup starts while everyone else finished setting up their starting blocks. The announcer stepped to the line, "Runners, take your mark." Everyone did their own routine and got into their blocks. I stretched out my right leg, then my left before placing them in the blocks. I swayed once to the right and once to the left. "Everybody up! Everybody up!" the announcer said. We looked at him after we all got out of the ready positions in the starting blocks to see what the problem was. His next statement, "I need everyone to get in their blocks and hold your heads down. That will tell me that you are ready." Everyone nodded to let him know that we understood what he had said. The announcer started again, "Runners, take your mark." I repeated the same actions as before. My heart started beating fast. "Seeeet!" "Come on, bra," I said to myself. Boom! The gun sounded. I shot out of the blocks. Hurdle one □ hurdle two□ Meridian is out in front, hurdle three □ hurdle four, "Come on, let's go," I thought □ hurdle five □ hurdle six, "Hold your place." Hurdle eight □ hurdle nine □ hurdle ten. "Sprint . . . lean," I thought as I crossed the finish line. The top four finishers would be going to state, and I got fifth. No state in the high hurdles for me. From there, I had to go straight to pole vault. When I got there it was perfect timing, because they were just about to start. I was glad, because I could catch my breath. I didn't have to jump until 10 feet, 6 inches anyway, so I would be ready when the time came. I looked around and saw the jumpers I was competing with and knew I would win. When I did start vaulting, it was smooth sailing all the way up to 12 feet, 6 inches. At that height I scratched all three times. I just used it as a practice for state. I needed to find out where

I had to put my standards.

Next up was the 4 by 1, and I was the first leg. It was a photo finish, but we came in fifth. Then in the 4 by 2 we placed sixth. Then the event I had dreaded, the 300-meter hurdles. I just did not like running it. Coach Carter came up to me as I was heading to the starting line, "We are tied for second. You can't get anything less than fifth." When Coach said that, he hit me with some pressure. He put winning or losing on my back, even though we still had the mile relay. I had to sprint the whole race. "Runners, take your mark," the announcer said. I did my pre-race routine. Then got into the blocks, "Dang, man, I have to run the whole way," I whispered to myself. "Set," was the next word from the announcer. Boom! The gun sounded and we were off. I came out hard with my eyes fixed on the Meridian kid. I passed three guys in the straight. Once I got to the curve, the bear jumped on my back, but I fought to hold my position. In the straight I was in fifth place. "Let's go, Bryant!" I heard my team cheering me on. Twenty meters left in the race, and the third-place guy hit my last hurdle and made it crooked. When I saw that, I shook my head. When I got to the last hurdle, I just olayed it and finished the race. Coach Carter came to me a few minutes after the race and said, "Why did you do that? You may have been disqualified." "Coach," I said, "how was I supposed to jump the hurdle when it was crooked from someone else? There was no way I was going to take a chance on that. I don't practice jumping crooked hurdles." He shook his head and walked away from me. We won the mile relay and that gave us enough to win the meet. We were South State champions. We won by five points.

The next week, the only people who had to come to practice were the ones who qualified for state along with the alternate runners. I qualified for the pole vault, but Coach made me run so I guessed I was an alternate runner for the mile relay. I really just ran, because he told me to. I did not have any intention of actually running in that relay. So, I had hoped everyone would be good enough to run and after I did my one event I could be a spectator. When we left Friday afternoon, Coach Carter said he wanted us to get a good night's rest. The next day, we went to Pearl High School where the state track meet was held. We got there early enough so we could pick a good spot to set up our tent. Thirty minutes later they called for field event check-ins. The pole vault worker asked me what height I wanted to come in at. I looked down at the sheet and the lowest height you could come in at was 11 feet. I told him I would come in at 11 feet. Coach Pee walked up and said, "What height are you coming in at?" "Eleven," I said. "Isn't your PR 11 feet, 6 inches?" Coach Pee said. I chuckled, and said, "Yep! Shoot I might as well come in at a height I know I can get plus with this new pole I will be able to clear that with no problem." I was confident in that height, because I had cleared it. Everything else was a different story. I only cleared 12 feet in practice. Coach Pee looked at me with a reassuring face and said, "OK, good luck. I will be going back and forth checking on everyone, but I will get some pictures of you jumping."

I had hoped the pole vault coach would come that day, so I could ask him for some pointers. He had been helping me all year. They made an announcement for everyone to get their practice jumps in. As I attempted to go down the runway, I was bit nervous and I bailed out of the jump. "Scoot the standards back five numbers," I heard the voice of the Ocean Springs coach say and turned around with a smile on my face. I went over to greet him as I waited for my second practice run. Next time, I moved the standards to twenty-five like he had said and went over just fine. I had a feeling that I would have to push them back as the day went on. For that moment, I was going to stick with that. The runway was then closed because we were about to start shortly. I went over to Coach Carter and explained how different the standards were from back home. There were only three people who were coming in at 11 feet. Everyone else was coming in at 13 feet. "Lavender on deck," said the guide, who was working the pole vault. When it was my turn, I made sure my standards were set on twenty-five. I walked back to my starting position and stared down the pit. I focused in on what I needed to do. I pumped myself up and took off down the runway. Pink! That was the sound as I stuck the pole into the pit. I pulled down, pointed my toes, did my rotation and let go of the pole. When I hit the mat, I knew I had cleared it. I went over to the Ocean Springs coach and asked, "What do you think?" "Well," he said, "I think you need to push your standards back another three. I say that because you came in with so much speed." "Yeah, I did, huh," I normally didn't come in with that much speed, because I would be coming from the hurdles. I walked over and told Coach Carter the adjustment, and he just nodded his head. The next time, my standards would be at twenty-eight. I cleared 11 feet, 6 inches easily. Twelve feet was next up and I kept my standards the same for that height. I had never attempted a 12 foot height in a meet. It would be a new PR for me once I cleared that height. When my turn came, I scratched the first time, but the second time I pulled down on the pole harder to get more flex in the pole. That was all I needed to clear it, a new PR. The next height was 12 feet, 6 inches. I was a little nervous, because I had never attempted that height. I walked over to Coach Pee and said, "I'm nervous." "Why?" she asked. "Because I've never been that high, and this pole isn't that flexible," I said. "Ah, boy!" she said. "Go jump that height." I just smiled and went over to get some pointers from the Ocean Springs coach. I adjusted my hand grip as I went to my starting mark on the runway. I did my starting routine and took off; because I was nervous I was coming in hot. I reached the pit, stuck the pole in the pit, pulled hard, rotated, and let the pole go. As I made my way down, I hit the bar. I had to scoot my standards closer. I repeated my normal routine, but that time pulled down even harder when I hit the pit and it gave me just enough room to clear the height. My new PR was now 12 feet, 6 inches.

The next height was 13 feet; I looked at Coach Carter and shook my head. He didn't argue with me. He just nodded his head. He came back with, "Bryant, you will be on the 4 by 4." In my head I already knew that was coming for some reason and said, "For real? Coach, you know I don't like that race." "I know," he said, "but the team needs you, so you are running." I just shook my head and went to where my other teammates were competing so I could cheer them on. When it was time to line up for the race, I was thinking, "Dang! I don't want to run this race." Pow! The gun went off. I was after Dallas. He was second, and I was third leg. He stepped on the track and when he got the stick I stepped on the track. Here comes Dallas, "Come on, B! Let's go," I heard my teammates yell out. "Stick," Dallas yelled out. I reached back to get the stick. I took off. The first hundred I was great, the second one I was decent, and the third is when the bear jumped on my back. I fought through that and now for the last straight. I could not feel my legs as I got to the end of that stretch. I handed off the stick and fell off the track on to the ground. I couldn't move anything at all. That was the hardest I had ever run a four hundred meter. "Bryant, get up," Dallas said when he came over. I didn't move at all. "Bryant, come on, bra. Get up," he said. "I can't," I said. "I have no more energy." He laughed while helping me up. "Aye," I said. "I really can't feel my legs so walk with me for a minute." When we got back to the team area, Coach Pee said, "Boys, y'all did great. I think that was the fastest y'all ever ran." We finished fifth that year at the state meet. I was happy because there would be no more left turns for a year.

Questions

1. How many times have people told you to change your dream because they do not see you being successful?

2. How did you handle the success God let you have despite what everyone said?

3. Do you see the greatness in yourself?

CHAPTER 5

Breakthrough:
After Busting Through the Barrier, Then You Notice Small Cuts

SOUTH ALABAMA DAY CAMP

Two weeks after the school year ended I received a phone call from Tim Elbow. He was a local referee who had called my games since I was in peewee football. I answered the phone, "Hello?" "Hey, Bryant, it's Tim Elbow. Have you heard of the University of South Alabama?" "No, sir." "Well they are starting a football program over there in Mobile. You need to go to the camp they are having this Saturday." "Where is that?" I said. "I don't even know where the school is." "Call Coach Coe," he said. "He will know what I'm talking about. He will take you. I would, but I have a family trip planned. I just think you need to go. You are too good of a player not to get a shot to play D1 ball." "OK," I said, "is there a coach that I can contact for more information on the camp?" "Yes," he said, "but it is against the rules right now. There is a coach by the name of Dean Kilo. Coach Coe knows him." "OK," I said, "thank you so much." I hung up the phone and called Coach Coe. "Hey, Coach," I said, "I just got a call from the referee Tim Elbow. He said there is a school, University of South Alabama, starting a football team. Have you heard anything about that?" "Really?" Coach Coe said, "So South Alabama is finally doing it. Well I haven't heard anything about it. What else did he say?" "He told me to tell you to call Dean Kilo, that you know him," I said. "Oh, I know Dean," he said, "met him years ago when I coached at Moss Point. Let me give him a call and see what is going on." "OK," I said. "Tim said they have a camp Saturday." "Bryant," Coach Coe said, "I will find everything out and call you back in ten minutes. Stay by the phone." I sat by the phone and waited for Coach to call back. About ten minutes later he called me back. "What's up, Coach?" "All right," he said, "Dean has confirmed that there is a camp on Saturday." I jumped up with excitement and said, "Coach, can you take me?" "Well, I don't know; let me check with my wife. Did you ask your Mom?" "Yes, sir, she already said that she could not take me," I really just wanted Coach to take me because we were already successful one time with the Scout/Under Armor combine, and I wanted to see if we could go for a second successful time together. "OK, I will call back by the end of the day," Coach said. I did not have any plans that day, so I played the NCAA football video game all day, too excited to do anything other than wait on that call for Coach to tell me what time we were going to the camp.

Coach Coe called back around 5 p.m., "Hey, Bryant. Did you see what time the camp starts?" "Yes, sir, it starts at 10 a.m. held at this stadium called Ladd Peebles," I said with a confused voice. "Yeah, I know. That stadium is where the senior bowl is held every year." "Oh, OK," I said. "I'll pick you up about 8:30 a.m.," he said. "Make sure you get a good night's rest." "Yes, sir," I replied to him and for the rest of the day I just thought about the opportunity I would be getting in the morning. I got all my gear together and put it in a book bag as soon as we got off the phone. Then I continued to play the college football video game to keep me calm. When my Mom came home from work, I went into the den to tell her the great news. "Mama, I got invited to this camp in Mobile, Alabama. It is for this school University of South Alabama. Have you heard of that school before?" My Mom shook her head and said, "No, never heard of it. Is their football team good?" "Well," I said, "they have never had a team before. This will be the first season this fall." "Oh, OK," she said. "So they heard about you?" "No," I said. "I heard about them. One of the referees called me and told me about their camp. I called Coach Coe, because he knows a little bit of everyone." "Is Coach Coe going to take you to this camp, too?" she said. "Yes, Ma'am," I said. "He said he would pick me up at 8:30 tomorrow morning because the camp starts at 10." "OK, cool," Mom said. "Do you have all your stuff you need?" "Yes," I replied. "I already packed my bag with all my stuff. I'm ready to go right now." We both chuckled a little bit. After that, I just hung out with my little brother for a while and played the football video game until I went to bed.

The next morning when my alarm woke me up, I got up, put on my clothes and went to the kitchen to get a bowl of cereal before Coach showed up. My Mom walked out of her room, and said, "Morning baby." "Morning, Mama," I said after taking my first bite of cereal. "Do you have all your stuff together?" "Yes, Ma'am, it is over by the door like last time." "OK, are you going to take a Gatorade with you?" "Yes, I have one in the freezer," I said. "OK," she said, "what time is Coach coming to pick you up?" I finished drinking the milk from my bowl of cereal, and I saw Coach pull up at the same time, "Right now," I said in answer to my Mom. I put my bowl in the sink, headed for the door, scooped up my book bag, and yelled, "Mama, I'm gone." "OK, good luck," she yelled back as I was shutting the front door. I opened the car door and said, "Good morning. Coach. How are you?" "Morning, Bryant, and the question is, how are you? Did you get some rest last night?" I laughed at his response, "Yes, sir." "Good," he responded. As we headed down Cowan/Lorraine Road and east on I-10 toward Mobile. That ride kind of felt like the last ride we had taken except I knew what to expect a little bit. He had on his ESPN radio like always, and I began to immerse myself in my thoughts. This was a little different from the last time because I knew that one of two things could happen that day. One, I would catch a coach's eye, and he would offer me a scholarship. Two, I would catch a coach's eye, and he would come watch me and later on offer me a scholarship. In my eyes either way they were going to offer me. I just did not know when it would be. The ride with Coach was completely quiet until we got into Mobile. Then Coach started with his disclaimer like he did when we went to New Orleans. Only this time it was more harsh speech. "Now, look," he said, "you are not going over there just for the fun of it. You are going to show these coaches what you can do, to possibly see if they will give you a scholarship. This is business!" "Yes, sir," I replied while smiling. I felt the adrenaline pumping through my body. "I told Dean about you, so he will be looking for you. I vouched for you; I told him you were a player. Don't make me regret this. Go do what you have been coached to do." "Yes, sir. I gotcha, Coach," I answered with a coolness in my voice, but in the back of my mind I knew there was a lot at stake. I could fulfill one dream of many I have had since I was a little boy.

We got out of the car and walked to where the other athletes were walking into the stadium. Coach Dean walked up, and said, "Coe, what are you doing here?" He was around the same age as Coach Coe. I analyzed the man. I could see he was full of life and very energetic. "Well, Dean. Remember the young man I told you about on the phone," said Coach Coe, pointing at me. "I brought him over so you can take a look at him." Coach Dean's eyes were locked on me as he walked over, "Dean Kilo," he said. "Bryant Lavender," I answered as we shook hands. "Coe tells me you play receiver. Can you catch it?" he said. "Yes, sir." I replied. "He says you remind him a receiver he coached at Moss Point by the name of Donnie Prune, now he was a player. So, you are that good, huh?" I smiled, "I can hold my own, Coach." Coach Dean smiled, "We will see today." "Yes, sir," I said while smiling. "Bryant, I think you have to go sign in," Coach Coe said. As I turned around and started heading to the tent I heard Coach Dean say, "Coe, can he really play?" I laughed to myself about his question. "I'm about to show you how good I can play," I thought as I walked to the tent. I scanned the area to view the competition I would be going against. As I began to warm up I glanced over the stadium to see where I could be playing for the next four or five years of my life. We were then called up, introduced to the whole coaching staff, and then broken up by position. "It's time to ball," I said to myself as all the other receivers and I jogged over to our spot. This was when we really found out a little bit about Coach Jeno. "What's up? "My name is Coach Jeno. I played at the University of Auburn, played in Canada for a few years and finished my career with the Carolina Panthers. This means a lot for me to coach here, because I am a Mobilian. I played high school ball at Blount. I'm going to be real with y'all; I'm only bringing in ballers. So, if you are a baller, then ball out. It is just that easy." After that introduction, it gave me a weird feeling. It was either you make plays or I find someone else who will. After that, we went over a few routes that would be in South Alabama's playbook. He took us through the curl, dig and comeback route. He threw us all the routes while the quarterbacks warmed up their arms. In routes on air we started off with the curl route. "QBs don't come over here messing up my drill or I will send you somewhere else," Coach Jeno said while demonstrating how he wanted the ball thrown. "Throw it just like that," was the next thing he said. That made me kind of nervous, because he threw the ball so hard it went through the hands of the receiver he was demonstrating with.

We all got three reps at each route before we went into one-on-one's with the defensive backs. Coach Stone called everyone up before a rep was taken in that drill, "Now we are about to compete. We are about to see how good you really are. Everyone stay up, but show us why you belong here at South Alabama. The DBs and receivers will be over here on the fifty going in. The O-line and D-line will be on the opposite side in the end zone." Everything started to speed up, whistles were blowing, and athletes were jumping in line trying to show their talent off. The energy of the camp escalated. Some guys were talking noise about what they were going to do in that period. I didn't say anything, just got in line and prepared myself for my turn. Coach Dean walked up to me and said, "Bryant can you play outside and slot?" "Yes, sir," I replied as I secured my position in line as the third receiver up. When it was my turn up, the quarterback gave me a slant route. The defensive back was in off-man coverage so I knew it would be fairly easy to win on this route. "Hut!" One, two, three stick, and I made my break and stayed strong as the defensive back grabbed my wrist. I made the catch and gave a burst upfield. I jogged the back to the quarterbacks, "Bryant, get right here. Run a twelve yard out," said Coach Dean putting me in the slot position. I skipped everyone and got to the front of the line. As I lined up this time the defensive back was in my face. I gave him a single stick release and got off the line. I kept him on my right hip, and gave him a one, two at the top of my route as I broke to the sideline. The quarterback threw it a little high, and the defensive back had good position. He put his hands up, but it didn't matter because I jumped over him, snatched the ball out of the air and held on to it as I came out of the air.

I jogged the ball back in and got in line. I was waiting on my turn to go again when coach Dean said, "Bryant, go outside. Run a curl." I nodded and jumped up to the line. The defensive back is manned up again. "Hut!" I speed released that time, dropping my right shoulder and ripping through his arms. He thought I was running a go on him. When I broke down at twelve yards, he kept going. The quarterback delivered the ball, and it was an easy catch with no one around me. All you could hear was, "Oooooooooo," from the other athletes watching as they were awaiting their turns. When I jogged back some of the athletes gave me a compliment on the route I had just run. I went to the back of the line because I needed to find some water. When I came back from getting water, Coach Stone had blown the whistle and said, "Coaches, pick a player you want to represent you. This would be the best-on-best showdown. They would only get one rep." When Coach Stone stopped talking, everyone stayed quiet waiting to get picked by a coach. "Bryant, you know I'm going with you right," Coach Dean said. I just smiled and walked over by him. "What route do you want to run?" Coach Dean asked. I said, "Post corner," immediately. He looked at the quarterback, "You OK with that?" He nodded his head yes. "Seven three," I told him so we would be on the same timing. I gave him a pound, then went to line up.

As I walked up to the line and got settled into my stance, there was a little bit of tension. Not between the defensive back and me, but amongst the coaches, like they had been waiting for this matchup all day. This was the matchup they had been wanting to see. This would tell them if I was able to play at the next level. The defensive back was in bump-and-run technique. He was head up, with a slight inside leverage. "A'ight, bra! What you go'n' do?" I thought. "If you go inside with that leverage he could wash you down or you could get tangled up when you break to the corner. Go outside, bra." I looked the defensive back in the eyes then looked inside at the ball. "Hut!" I came off the ball, gave him a single stick release, and went outside. He was playing my hip, so he allowed me to get half a body in front of him. That was perfect position for me to do what I wanted to do. I broke to the post, looked at the quarterback to sell the post route. The defensive back jumped it, and as soon as he did that I broke to the corner while giving him a chicken wing at the top to finish him off. As I looked back to track the ball I noticed that I had to leave my feet. I took three more steps and then took flight as I watched the ball fall right into my hands. I hit the ground, ball secured, and the catch made. When I got up, the whole camp exploded. Everyone ran to me to congratulate me. In the midst, I glanced over at Coach Coe to see his body language, to see if he approved. He gave me the nod that he liked what had just happened and all I could do was smile. After the rowdiness started to calm down, the defensive back came up to me and shook my hand. I knew he respected me for doing that first-class move. Shortly after that, Coach Stone blew the whistle and had his closing remarks of the camp.

"Everyone did a great job today," Coach Stone said. "That is the way you compete. I thank every one of you for coming out today and showing us what you can do. We have all you guys' numbers. We will contact you to let you know if we want to see you again. Please, be safe on the road, and, again, thank you for coming out." After that, we broke it down on Jaguars. The athletes began to scatter, and I headed in the direction where I left my book bag. "Bryant! Bryant!" Coach Dean was calling my name. I turned around, "Sir?" "Do not go anywhere yet," he said. "Matter of fact, meet me at the fifty-yard line. I have someone that I want you to meet." I looked for Coach Coe and found him down by the entrance, and I pointed that I had to go to the middle of the field. He nodded his head that he understood what I was saying. When I got there, I saw Coach Dean and Coach Stone talking to another athlete. I just waited until they finished up. Coach Dean turned and looked at me, "Bryant, this is Coach Stone." I reached out and shook his hand. "Thanks for coming out today. You did a great job. You competed and that's what we are looking for here at South Alabama," Coach Stone said. "Thank you, Coach," I replied. "Someone raised you right; I can see that by the way you carry yourself. Who raised you? Mama and Daddy? Grandma? Aunt?" "My Mother," I simply said. "Well, you tell her she did a great job with raising you. Are you an only child?" "No, sir, I am the middle child of three boys." Coach Stone nodded with a smile. Next, both of them looked at one another and back at me. "Bryant, on behalf of Coach Stone and myself, along with the University of South Alabama, we would like to offer you a full athletic scholarship." I couldn't believe what I had just heard. He just offered me a scholarship to go to school and play ball. I started to get weak; my knees buckled a little bit. My face had shock all over it, "Thank you, Coach! I I I" Coach Dean cut me off, "Look you don't have to commit today. We are just letting you know that we want you to come be a Jaguar. I will be in touch with you soon. Tell Coe to call me tonight." I shook their hands and walked away at the same time, trying to control my excitement – controlling myself professionally like Coach Coe had stressed to me. My mind was going crazy, "They just offered me a scholarship. They really just offered me a scholarship." That was all I could think about.

As I got to Coach Coe, I said, "Coach Dean said to call him tonight." "OK," Coach Coe said. "Hey, what did they say to you on the fifty?" "Let's get in the car first," I replied. "I don't want to say out here." Coach Coe's eyes lit up, and we got to the car in double time. We began to pull out of the parking lot; I had played the conversation in my head about ten times already. "OK, Coach," I said, "when Coach Dean told me to go to the middle of the field, he introduced me to Coach Stone. Then they offered me a full scholarship." Coach Coe threw the car in park, turned and looked me in the eyes and said, "Are you serious?" "Yes, Coach. 'On behalf of Coach Stone and me, along with the University of South Alabama, we would like to offer you a full athletic scholarship,'" I said. "Were those the exact words, Bryant?" he asked. "Yes, Coach. So, what do I do now?" I asked. "Did you commit?" he said. "No, sir." "Well," he said, "you can't tell anybody yet, because they can change their mind. Just wait until you get the paper in the mail. You can share it with your family if you want, but I wouldn't tell anyone else." "No, Coach," I said. "I'm not telling anyone, won't even tell my family. I will let them read the paper when it comes in the mail." "All right," Coach Coe said, "that sounds good to me." "Coach, how do you think I performed?" I asked. "Well, I think you performed great. You showed the coaches that you would do whatever it takes to make a play. When you dove for the ball on that post corner, you showed that you would leave your feet. That sealed the deal in my mind. That was why they offered you." I smiled at that statement from my Coach. "Bryant, everything changes now that you have an offer on the table," Coach Coe said. "Now, when someone comes to talk to you, it is, what can, or what are, they offering you. Now you are trying to figure out if they will match what South Alabama did. If they do, then it is a matter of where do you want to go, and do the schools that offered you currently have great educational ratings. That is the most important thing, because you can go anywhere and play ball. The final thing to look at would be does this school fit you, can you go there and be successful."

His words gave me so much to think about, I was still overwhelmed from the things that had transpired. The rest of the ride home, I just thought about how it would be playing for South Alabama. When we pulled up to my house I looked at coach and smiled. "Thank you, Coach, for everything," I uttered as I threw my book bag over my shoulder. "You are welcome, Bryant. You did the work. I'm just glad to be a part of it. Call me if you hear anything else from Coach Dean or anyone else from South Alabama." "Yes, sir," I said shutting the door. When I entered the house my Mama was in the den. "What's up, Mama?" I said trying to stay composed and hide everything. "Hey, B, how did the camp go?" "It went great. I did really well," I said, still trying to hide the fact that I got offered a scholarship. She just smiled and said, "I knew you were going to do the darn thing. Can't anybody mess with my baby. You are the best!" I smiled because she was speaking purely from her heart without knowing that her baby got a scholarship for school. She left to go to the bathroom, and I snuck out of the room so she wouldn't ask me any more questions about the camp. Or else I would end up telling her what had happened.

SENIOR YEAR

The rest of the summer I did not go to any more individual camps. Because we had a new coach and the summer lifting program was the worst one I had ever been a part of. A few of us did extra lifting and running on our own. We knew we were not going to get stronger doing the same full body complex exercises they instructed us to do. So, we designated days when we squatted, benched and dead-lifted. We also made the underclassmen we knew that would see a lot of playing time stay to get the workout with us.

Two weeks before fall camp started, I received my official scholarship letter in the mail. My Mom placed our mail on the table for us, and when I saw the envelope with the official school heading on it, I got a bit excited. I ripped the top open and pulled the folded letter out of the envelope. I unfolded the paper, and it read:

"Dear Bryant,
You have been offered a full athletic scholarship to play football at the University of South
Alabama.... etc."

That was all I could read was the opening sentence because tears began to run down my face. I walked into the den where my Mom was, "Boy what are you crying for?" she said. I handed her the letter so she could read it for herself. I watched her put her reading glasses on, and I wiped my face as I waited for her reaction after reading what the letter said. In about fifteen seconds, "Heeeeeeeyyyyyyy! Ain't gotta pay for anything, do you hear me?" she said and jumped off the couch, giving me a high-five and a hug. She had a smile from ear to ear and then she went straight to the phone to call everybody, to inform them that her baby had gotten a scholarship for school. I left the room, because I had to make one call myself. I pulled my phone out and dialed Coach Coe's number. "Hello?" "Hey, Coach," I said. "It came in the mail today." "What came in the mail today?" he asked. "My official scholarship letter from South." "Oh, it did?" he said. "Good! That means they were serious about wanting you. You didn't commit or anything did you?" "No, sir," I replied, "I was going to wait a little bit to see what other schools are interested in me." "OK," he said, "that is not a bad idea. Just don't wait too long because they can take the offer back." "Yes, sir." I said. "You ought to call Coach Dean," Coach Coe said, "and let him know that the official letter came in the mail." "OK," I said. "I will do that when we get off the phone." "Well," he said, "go ahead and call him now." "Yes, sir." I got off the phone and dialed Coach Dean's number. I was nervous to talk to him. "Hello, Coach Dean," he said, answering his phone. "Hey, Coach, it's Bryant. I just wanted to let you know I got the official scholarship letter in the mail today." "Awesome," he said. "I was wondering about that. I'm glad you got it." "Look, Coach," I said. "I really appreciate you all giving me the opportunity to get an education and play ball." "Oh, you don't have to thank me," he said, "you earned it. I know you can play, I saw it when you came to the camp. Coe told me that you could play, and he has always given me players. I'm just glad we saw you before someone else did." "I thank you, Coach," I said. "Listen, Bryant, don't thank me," Coach Dean said. "You just show me how thankful you are when you finish up your senior year and come be a Jaguar." I didn't say anything because if I had, it would have been giving him a soft verbal. "Look," he said, "you do not have to commit right now. We know that we were your first offer and when people start reevaluating, you will get some offers. Enjoy the process, take everything in and when you are ready to commit, make sure it is the right fit," he said. "Yes, sir." I replied. "I just hope that the right fit is a Jaguar," he said. We both laughed at his last statement and got off the phone. For a moment he didn't try to sell me on the school he was coaching. He didn't try to sell me a dream. That was pure honesty.

Everyone I was directly connected to did not know I had been offered a scholarship at that point. The only people who knew were my family and best friends. That Sunday

I planned on sharing it with my church family. When I got to church early I saw Pastor Gee, went up to him, shook his hand and gave him a hug. "Pastor, look, read this please," I said. He took the envelope, pulled the letter out and began to read it. Immediately he started smiling, stood from the stool and gave me a high five. "Son, this is what you have been waiting for right here," he said. "God answered one of your prayers. Have you praised him yet?" "Pastor," I said, "I have been praising Him since it came in the mail. I haven't committed yet, because it is early but once I get done praising Him, what do I do next?" "Amen to that, son," he said. "Once you have come down off your spiritual high, ask God if this school is where you need to be. Even though God blessed you with this offer how do you know more are not coming?" He chuckled.

That day his sermon was exactly what I needed to hear. It was about God blessing you with opportunities, and you having enough faith in God to allow Him to pick which opportunity to take. For example: there are three opportunities you have and you know they are from God. So, no matter which one you pick you will be blessed. Question: will you allow God to pick the opportunity that He wants you to have to maximize His kingdom? Wisdom: When you allow God to choose which opportunity not only will you grow His kingdom, but He will maximize the blessing of the job.

At the end of service Pastor Gee announced to the rest of the congregation that I had received a scholarship from South. Everyone clapped and gave me a hug; it was amazing to feel the love from outside my immediate family. That also got me thinking later that day about what all happened from the past week. Tears started to escape my eyelids and trickled down my face as I began to speak to my Dad. "Well, Dad, I kept one of my promises. I will be playing on TV just like I told you I would. Now I have one more promise to do. Just let me get this one done first. I need you to stay close to me like you've been. Dang, Daddy! I wish you were physically here. To see that smile on your face would be awesome. Daddy, I love you." I continued to cry until I fell asleep.

The next day I received a text from Coach Coe saying to call Coach Dean. So, I called him, "Hey, Bryant," Coach Dean said. "I can't call you right now because we are in what you call a dead period. So, if a recruiter wants to talk to the player you have to call me. So, did you have a good camp? Are you healthy?" "Yes, sir, I did, and I am," I said. He replied, "I will probably come see you the first week of the season. If not the first week then I will be there second week for sure." "OK, Coach," I said, "sounds good." "Bryant," he said, "I have to run. We are having a staff meeting in few minutes. I will call you sometime next week." Just like that, Coach Dean was gone.

After the season started I had a bit of an uneasy feeling about Coach Banks, because he was not following through with some of the things he had said to me. But what do I know? Coaches coach, and players play so all I could do was what I was told. We went from having a high-speed, no-huddle spread offense to the traditional old-school power I. I expressed to Coach Banks some things that were bothering the seniors, but he showed little to no interest in those things. He seemed not to care about my class. He was just implementing his new system, preparing the younger guys for next year. He told the seniors we had control, that he would allow us to do things, but why did we believe him? Was it just a lie? We were expressing our thoughts to him because he encouraged us to do so. The only reason we did those things was to put us in a position to go to the playoffs, to compete in December for the state championship.

About four weeks into the season what he had promised me when we had first met in the cafeteria was not coming to fruition. I realized then that he had just given me lip service. I wanted to confront him about it, but I decided not to, because we had a decent record. I didn't want to go to him and remind him what he had told me, because it would have made me look like a selfish player. At that point in the season not many people at school knew, other than my cousins Kevin, Oliver and one of my best friends, Bernard, that I had a scholarship to South Alabama.

One day during school I got called to the field house to speak with Coach Feeney. He was the head coach at Mississippi Gulf Coast Community College, also known as Perk by locals on the Mississippi Gulf Coast. I walked into the field house. Coach Feeney turned around and said, "Bryant, how are you son?" "I'm well, Coach," I said. "How are you?" "I'm great. Thanks for asking," he replied. "I wanted to talk with you and see where your head is about school, because we want you to come be a Bulldog. You know that, right?" I just smiled when he said that and said, "Well, Coach, I started to wonder if you all wanted me. Honestly, Coach, I am a bit surprised you all didn't come speak with me sooner." The look on his face was poised and calm. I was playing the game just like he was. He knew that EMCC had come to speak with me, and I could tell he was not worried about them. I mean, Perk was the big-dog on campus so to speak. I knew all about them and also Jerry, one of my best friends, was going there. "Well, Bryant," he said, "you know us. We are going to win. I know the Lions came and spoke with you, but, listen, it's in the middle of nowhere. Hours away from your family, and they won't treat you better than we will at Gulf Coast. Come be a Bulldog." I looked him very calmly in the eyes and said, "What do I bring to your team that you don't already have?" I asked that question because he was right, I knew a lot about them. I looked at which receivers went to them. They literally had a stack. That question caught him off guard, but he kept a composed look on his face. Now I was waiting for his sales pitch. "Well," he said, "you have playmaking ability, speed on the outside to stretch the field. You are a sure-hand wideout. You are just a pure playmaker, and we need that. We need you." "OK, Coach," I said, "I will talk it over with my parents." "Bryant, that sounds good," he said. I shook his hand and went back to class not believing anything he had just told me. Perk didn't need me. He was just selling me, because he really didn't want to play against me. I was already hip to the kind of things coaches might tell me, thanks to Coach Coe being in my corner and sharing his knowledge about recruiting with me.

As the season went on, we found our way into the playoff hunt. Pascagoula was the game that would determine if we would make the playoffs. That game would be a defensive game. Offensively we were going back and forth with three and outs. It was time for a big play from our team, and I was determined to make it. I was back to receive the punt, it was the third quarter and the score was seven all. This would be the defining moment of the game; it was time to make a big play. I set up about thirty-five yards away from the line of scrimmage waiting for the punter to kick the ball. The referee blew the whistle to start the clock. Boom! I saw the ball in the air seconds after it was snapped. I tracked the ball in the air and locked my eyes on it. I saw out of my peripheral vision that I would be able to run with the ball instead of making a fair-catch signal. "Relax and do what you do," I said to myself right before the ball came into my arms. I burst up field, made one miss, then broke toward Pascagoula's sideline. Just before I could turn the corner a defender jumped to tackle me and I used my left arm to stiff arm him off of me. As I used my strength to break the tackle he had the back side of my shoulder pads. When I pushed, I gave a dead leg to make him let go, but he had a good grip, and my right foot got stuck in the ground. I felt it give way as I did the unsuccessful elusive move. He fell off of me, but I still fell to the ground after a few yards. When I stood up after that play something was wrong with my right ankle. It did not feel the same. It felt loose, and I couldn't push off of it. I thought it was just from the numb feeling so I stayed on the field. The next play was a running play, so I had a chance to check it out when I took off but when I pushed, nothing happened. I hopped off of the field and went straight to the trainer. "I need you to re-tape me as tight as you can so I can go back out there," I told the trainer. "Wait, Bryant, what happened?" he said. I kind of rolled my eyes a bit as I told him what had happened during my punt return. He started to palpitate my ankle while asking if it hurt. My answer was no until he got right above my lateral malleolus. I jumped a little, "Yeah, that hurt," I said. "When you re-tape me make sure you tape that area tight." He gave me a blank face but reached for the tape anyway. When he got done taping me, I looked at him for my next instruction on what to do. "You have to run and let me see how you look while running." I got off the table and started to run, and I had to admit my ankle started to hurt when I would push off in the plantar flexion position. He told me to stop and before he said anything I asked, "Before you say 'No,' can you do the figure eights a few more times?" He nodded. The trainer did what I asked him, but it felt like he did not get it any tighter. He finished. I got off the table and started to run again, my ankle started to hurt even more, and I had to limp now. I came back to the training table, "Bryant, I don't," was all he could say before I started crying. That game was over for me. He took the tape off my ankle; put an ice bag on it. I sat on the bench and buried my face in my hands. I just cried, because I didn't know how bad it was. I didn't know if I could finish my season with my team. "After I have been selfless all season, taking care of the team goal and encouraging everyone else, God, why me?" I asked. "How come I have to get hurt? I always try to do the right thing even when no one is watching. I literally try to do everything right. What if this injury is season-ending? God, what if they take my scholarship? How will I help my family? Help me understand, because I don't." After the questions I asked God, I dried my face and looked up and my teammates were giving me their encouraging words. I saw on their faces that they didn't know what to do. I even overheard them say, "Bryant, hurt? We really not going to win now." I just sat there pouting and being selfish until I heard Ms. Kindle's voice. "Bryant! Bryant! Bryant!" she yelled, and I turned around to look back at her. She was giving me the hand motion to get up. I shook my head and turned back around. It was my moment to be selfish; I did not have the strength to pretend right now. I was hurting mentally. "Bryant Lavender, get your butt up and stop feeling sorry for yourself," Ms. Kindle said, her voice was really close. I turned around, and she was right behind me. She had sneaked her way onto the field. I ignored her command, "What are you doing? Why are you not on field?" "Bryant Lavender, did you hear what I said? Why are you over sitting on the bench pouting and crying like a little girl?" she said with a disappointed motherly tone. "I really don't feel like hearing anything encouraging right now," I said ignoring her attempts to get me off the bench. "Bryant Lavender," she said, "that is pure nonsense; whatever you do they do. You are a leader and the people following you are lost right now, because their leader is being selfish and got a little butt hurt over an injury. You are young, your body will heal. Inspiring these kids to be great only happens once." "Ugh! OK, Ms. Kindle, I will get up," I said in response to her statement. "Bryant, you can make it without football," she said. "Some of these other kids won't. So, if you quit today because some dang stupid injury, they will think it is OK to quit life when it gets hard. Now drink this PowerAde, get your butt off the bench and go be a dang leader for your team." "Yes, ma'am," I said.

That short, powerful conversation made me snap back to reality. I finished drinking the PowerAde and got my mind right to encourage my team. When I started to be a leader and encourage my teammates, the team morale rose tremendously. For the rest of the game I walked up and down the sideline reassuring my team. Although we lost by three points, I learned we must continue to push even in times of pain when the things we want most are cut down . When we have all the chips on the table, when we have everything to lose, God wants to know whether we still trust Him.

After we got on the bus, I thought, "What is really wrong with my ankle? And if I had not been selfish for those few moments would we have won?" I would always retrace my plays and emotions from that game to see what I could do better for the next game. I turned my phone on after I got settled in my seat on the bus, and I saw that I had quite a few missed calls and texts. I assumed it was because people found out that I had gotten hurt and did not return to the game. I had a message from Coach Pee, "Hey, B, I heard what happened. How bad is it?" I replied, "I don't know, they put it in the fast-cast thing. They said I need to go get an X-ray to check if it is broken." "Let me call Tabb," Coach Pee said, "and see if he will take X-rays for you." "OK," I replied. In about ten minutes my phone vibrated. It was a text from Coach Pee, "Tabb said to meet him at his private practice office tomorrow where he will take X-rays so he can see how to diagnose it. I will pick you up at 8 a.m." "OK, thanks, 'cause I can't go to school with this cast on my leg!" I responded. "Lol. Lol," she replied.

When I woke up the next morning I prayed for my ankle not to be broken or to have anything major wrong with it. When Coach Pee came to pick me up she looked at me with a half grin, "Boy, you don't know how to use crutches?" I shook my head and said, "And not trying to get good at using them." We both laughed as I got in the car. When we got to Mr. Tabb's private practice office, I was shocked because I didn't know he had one. It was in a nice building; we went around to the back so he could let us in. We walked in, went down a short hallway, took a left and that took us straight to the X-ray room. I hopped onto the table and he took my cast off. He palpitated my ankle to see what was swollen and what was still hurting. "Mr. Tabb, what do you think?" I asked, while he checked everything out. "Bryant, I don't know, honestly," he said. "We will have to wait until the X-rays show something. It may be broken." "Huh?" was my response just to make sure I had heard him correctly, but at the same time to spiritually in Jesus' name cancel any negativity implied by the mention of possible broken bones. He didn't repeat what he had said. "Bryant, do not move," he said. "Stay just like that. We are about to take a look." "Yes, sir," I replied. He placed my leg in specific position for the X-rays, took a few shots then came back and switched my ankle into a different position and took some shots. Then he put it in a third position and took the same amount of shots as he did for the first two. He didn't come back into the room after he had finished taking the shots. He was looking at the X-rays. Coach Pee and I just waited in the room for him to say something. I was trying to read his facial expressions, but I couldn't. After a few minutes of what in my head felt like years, he spoke over the intercom system, "Well, Bryant. It's not broken." "Thank you, Jesus!" I exclaimed from the table. Coach Pee started laughing because of my reaction. I knew she was happy for me though. "Y'all come in here, so I can show you what I see," Mr. Tabb said. Coach Pee helped me off the table and into the room where Mr. Tabb was. He was putting the X-rays on the wall, and I was looking at them, but all I could see was my tibia and fibula connected to my ankle. I didn't really see the problem until Mr. Tabb pulled down the middle picture and said, "You see this? This is your ankle. Right here is your tibia, and this is your fibula. Your fibula should not be that far apart. Normally with it being this far apart from the bottom part of the outside of our ankles it usually breaks. Although it is not broken we classify this injury as a high ankle sprain. Somebody has been praying for you, because your season was supposed to be over."

I smiled, thanked God, and the people who had been praying for me. "Bryant," he said, "you will be out for at least four-to-six weeks." "Mr. Tabb," I said, "is there any way I can come back any earlier?" I was not trying to miss that many games. "You need to do rehab at least two times a day for the next couple of weeks," he said. "Yes, sir. Is there anything I can do at home?" I asked. "Just ice it and maintain mobility," he said. "OK," I answered. There was no way that I was going to be out for whole month. "So, what about the cast, Mr. Tabb? Can I take it off and wear an ankle brace? I don't want to go to school with a cast on." "Come see me first thing Monday morning," he said, "and I will give you a special brace to wear." "Thank you, Mr. Tabb," I said.

The next day at church I hobbled inside with my crutches, and of course everyone wanted to know what had happened so I told them the story. The more I repeated the story the more I got discouraged that I would not come back fast enough to finish the season. During the service Pastor Gee was talking about connections and how he was connected to people he would never meet, because we in the congregation were connected to him; that we had to stay in God's will because there are specific people we are to be connected to who we have the ability to bring to the kingdom of God. There are people who he could not tell about God because his words carry no weight, but we can and will have a better chance because our name carries a weight in that world. Pastor Gee looked at me and said, "Son, you are going to do mighty things in the football world. You are a superstar, as long as you follow God's will for your life you will be one of the best players people will ever see. That will open up a door for people to ask you what the secret is, and you can simply give God the glory. God will open doors you thought were shut. He will make you play above your talent level. Stay in His will, son." When he said that it encouraged my spirit right on time. His words to me gave me strength to cancel out the doubt I was beginning to have. "Thank you, God," I whispered to myself.

The next morning, I got to school a little early so I could get the ankle brace Mr. Tabb had promised me Saturday. I did not have my cast on, but I walked slowly into the training room. Mr. Tabb had everything set up for me. "Bryant," he said, "ice your ankle for fifteen minutes before you put this on." "Yes, sir," I replied. That afternoon I went back to the training room during practice for my rehab to start. That hurt me so much because I did not like being in the training room. I was not supposed to be there. I belonged on the field. I felt so bad, because I could not do anything for my team. So, my goals for the next few weeks were to do the strenuous rehab, so I could finish the season with my teammates. I felt good about reaching my goals because that week was a bye and

I wouldn't miss much at practice.

Every day before school I was doing the non-exercise rehab, and after school I was doing pure movement rehab. That Wednesday I received some mail from Coach Dean. It was a square letter card that read:

"Bryant, It was sure good talking to you the other day. I hope your season is going well. When you get a chance give me a call."

-Coach Dean

A tear dropped down my face, and I got on my knees to pray to God. I asked Him if it was OK for me to verbally commit to the school. After about five minutes of talking with Him there was an unbelievable confidence in my spirit about giving South Alabama the verbal commitment. I walked into the den where my Mom was and I said, "Mama, I want to commit to South Alabama." "OK, baby," she said, "did you talk to Coach Coe about it?" "No, not yet," I said. "I am going to call him in a little bit." "OK," she said. "Well, whatever you want to do. I'm with you." I nodded and went into Za'Cari's room, "Aye, I'm going to commit this weekend." "For real?" he asked with excitement in his eyes. "Yeah," I replied confidently. "That's what's up, brody," he said. "Thanks," I said as I walked out of his room dialing Coach Coe's number. He didn't answer, but it didn't matter I would see him at school the next day anyway.

The next day before I could get down to his office he called me to his office. "What's up, Coach?" I said. "What's up with you?" he replied. "You called me yesterday. I missed your call, because I was busy making sure things were taken care of for the spring sports." "Oh, OK," I said. "I was just calling to tell you that I wanted to commit to South Alabama. I wanted your opinion on it before I made a move." "Well, first of all did you pray about it?" he said. "Second, what did your family say about it? Third, how do you feel about this decision?" I replied, "Yes I prayed about it. My family said to talk to you, and that whatever I decide they were behind me all the way. I feel great about the decision, honestly. I mean no other colleges have offered me a scholarship." "Wait," he said. "I thought East Mississippi and Perk spoke with you." "They did," I said, "but I don't want to go to a JUCO. My dream is to go straight to a university out of high school. Not saying there is anything wrong with going to a JUCO first. That is just a promise I made to myself." "That is a great goal to have," he said while placing his finger-tips together. "You have done what you need to do to set yourself up to have this opportunity. Think about more than football. You will get a great education from a great institution at South Alabama and that is what is most important. You can play ball anywhere, but you cannot get a great education anywhere. If you feel comfortable with your decision, then you know I'm with you. When are you going to give your verbal?" "This weekend," I said. "I am going to call Coach Dean on Saturday morning to give him the verbal." Coach Coe stood up, stuck out his right hand and said, "Well, Bryant, I am proud of you, son."

I shook his hand and said, "Thanks, Coach." He had a huge grin on his face when he said, "The easy part is over now, buddy." He finished that statement with a chuckle. I walked out of his office to go back to class. Now there was one more person I had to inform of my decision, Pastor Gee. I knew he would give me Godly counsel that I would need in this pivotal moment in my life. I was going to see him later on at Bible study.

That evening at church when I saw him, I walked right up to him. I didn't want to waste any time and said, "Pastor, I prayed, talked to my family and my Coach. I am going to commit to USA on Saturday." "Really? Wow, son," he said. "That's awesome. Go make a difference in the city of Mobile." "That's it?" I said. "Do you have any wisdom for me?" "Yeah, son," he said. "Stay good ground. If you stay good ground everything will fall into your hands." "Well, how do I do that?" I asked. "How do I stay good ground?" I had heard that term before but was not totally sure I knew what he was talking about. He answered, "You use the nuggets you have learned here and take them to Mobile. Once you get to Mobile plug into a church. Be a light in the city. Stay connected, make smart decisions, and understand why you are there. You are there to grow the Kingdom of God when success begins to take place. That is how you stay good ground in this season of your life." "Yes, sir," I said.

So, it was settled. I was going to the University of South Alabama to get an education while playing football. "When I call Coach Dean on Saturday to commit I hope he doesn't know anything about my ankle injury yet," I thought that Friday. I woke up about 9:30 a.m. the next morning and went to the den. "Ma!" I said. "I'm about to call Coach Dean and commit to South." With a huge smile on her face she said, "All right, Baby. You ready?' "Yep," I said. "I talked to everyone I needed to talk to. Talked to God, Coach Coe and Pastor Gee. Everything feels right. I don't have any second-guessing in my mind." "All right," she said, "call him and put it on speakerphone." I pulled out one of the handwritten letters he had sent to me, dialed the number and as it began to ring my heart started to beat fast. "Hello, Coach Dean," said the voice on the other end of the phone. "Hey, Coach, it's Bryant." "Hey, man!" he said. "How did the game go last night?" "Well, we had a bye, Coach. I have some news for you." "I hope it's good news," he said. "Lay it on me." "I'm coming, Coach," I said, and he responded, "Are you sure about that?" "Like I said, Coach, I'm coming. I'm ready to be a Jaguar." He let out a happy chuckle and said, "And we are glad to have you. This is the best news I have heard all week." "Coach, I just appreciate you for giving me an opportunity to play." "Bryant, you've earned it. You did it all at the camp. Coe said you could play, and you did not disappoint. Bryant, we are about to go into a staff meeting. I can't wait to share the good news with the rest of the coaching staff. I will call you back as soon as we get free. If it is late I will call you tomorrow." "Yes, sir!" I said. "Thanks again." I pressed end call on the phone and replayed the conversation in my head. I still was overwhelmed that I had a full scholarship to play football on the first football team the University of South Alabama would have.

When school started back Monday, the first person I told was my cousin Kevin. I had been riding with him to school every morning since he had gotten his car. "What's up, Cuz?" I said. "What did you do this weekend?" He shook his head and said, "Nothing, Cuz. All I did was work. You know me, I'm trying to stack my paper." "Yeah," I said, "I know and this was only the bye week, too. Wait until the football season is over. I'm surprised you don't smell like Mickie D's right now." We both let out a huge laugh before he answered back, "Forget you, Cuz. What did you do this weekend?" "Shoot, nothing," I said. "I can't go anywhere with a high ankle sprain." "Oh, yeah," he said. "I feel you. Aye, what did USA say about your ankle?" "Well, Cuz," I replied. "I don't think they know yet." "Huh?" he said. "You didn't tell them?" "Naw, Cuz," I said, "just like they offer. They can take it back. Plus, I don't want them to deem me as damaged goods." "Cuz," he said, "you know they are going to find out when they look at the stats and see you don't have any." "Cuz, I know," I replied. "That's why I'm coming back for the Harrison Central game. This week, we play Hancock. That will be an easy win." "OK, Cuz," he said, "but what are you going to do if they don't hold the offer?" "That's what I wanted to tell you, Cuz," I said. "I committed Saturday. I'm about to be a Jaguar." My cousin's face lit up with excitement for me, "Cuz!" he said. "For real? You committed?" I just nodded my head with a big smile on my face and said, "That's what's up, D1!" He yelled as we pulled into the school parking lot. "Cuz, you can't tell anyone," I said. "Let me tell everybody." "All right, Cuz," he said, "but what about the coaches. Are you going to tell them?" "Nope, forget them," I said. "They will find out when everyone else finds out. Right now, it's the people I know will be happy for me." He said, "Bet, I feel you on that." Throughout the rest of the day I told my friends Bernard, John, Jerry, Vincent and my little cousin Oliver. Those guys were who I was the closest with on the team. Everyone else would find out when my verbal would go public.

When I got home after practice I did a little extra of the new exercises that Mr. Tabb had showed me. I wanted to push my ankle so I could at least play against our school rivals in two weeks. I really didn't care to play this game against Hancock this week, because it would not do any good playing that game when it was a guaranteed win. My ankle made fantastic progress in the past week and a half. I could do dorsiflexion and plantar flexion completely without any pain, I could do eversion and inversion as well but had pain with those movements, and I could walk in my normal stride without any problems. Any cutting at this point created massive pain, though. When it got closer to game day everyone started asking me if I would be playing that week, and I just told them no because the last two weeks were more important.

On game day I got to the stadium early for treatment and in walked John. He hurt his neck the past week on a tackle; I assumed he was there for the same thing I was there for.

"What's up, John?" I said. "What's up, B?" he replied. "Nothing. I'm about to get the same thing you getting." "How are you feeling, bra?" I asked. "Man, better," he said, "but I will be glad when my neck loosens all the way up, and I can turn my head without twisting my whole body." I nodded my head and said, "Bet, I feel you on that." "How are you feeling, B?" he asked. "I'm feeling good, bra. I'm playing next week," I said, looking right over at Mr. Tabb to see if his body language changed, but it didn't. "For real, bra?" John said. "You already back at 100 percent?" I chuckled a little bit and said, "Naw, bra. Come on. Let's go to the field." I wrapped up my treatment and put my shoe back on. "Bra, I'm only about 65-70 percent, honestly," I said. "I can't cut for real, but I can go in a straight line." "Oh, OK," John said. "I gotcha. So, B, you are going to risk getting injured again? For high school?" "John," I said, "South doesn't know I'm injured. I haven't told them." "Why not?" he asked. "I'm afraid they will take the scholarship back and deem me as damaged goods," I said. "OK," he said, "I understand where you going with it now." "Yep, I replied, "and my ankle will be fully healed by the time I get to school there anyway. The other reason is just to keep the team morale up. Even if I can't do much they will play harder if they know I'm out there." "B," he said, "you are right. When you went down in the Pascagoula game that messed the team up." "We have a good team though, bra," I replied. "When one person goes down, the next one has to step up." John started laughing at me and said, "Come on, B. Man, don't do that. Talking about the next man has to step up, like there is another you waiting to get in. Bra, there is no next person. We need you on the offensive side of the ball, period." I couldn't help but laugh at what he had said.

I just didn't completely think that way because every coach I have ever had instilled and preached that there is no "I" in team — that one person does not make the team. If someone goes down, it was their job to prepare the next man to step in and take his place. I bought into the motto and never tried to look at it in a different way. When John explained it to me, I saw the difference in what he meant. As I watched the game that Friday, I saw it clearly. I wanted to tell my teammates little things to notice while they were on the field. That would give them an edge on the person they were going against. If they made a bad play, I would go encourage them, and that gave me an opportunity to pour more into my teammates than I ever have. It was the only thing I could do and still feel a part of the game without physically being in the game. I actually had a fun time being an encourager as I watched my teammates wreak havoc on Hancock, just like I knew they would. Easy win. Now, it was time to get ready for the next week because I was going to play. I had already made up in my mind that I was playing against the Rebels.

The next morning Coach Dean called me and the first words out of his mouth were, "Bryant, why didn't you play last night?" I looked up at the ceiling, because I really didn't want to tell him that I was hurt, but eventually I said, "I hurt my ankle last game, so the coaches wanted me to sit out this game because it would have been just a stat game for me." "How bad is it?" he said. "Not that bad," I replied. "They said it is a high ankle sprain. I will play this week for sure, Coach." "All right, big'n'," he said. "Just don't push yourself any more than you have to 'cause when you get here we want you healthy so you can play." "Yes, sir," I replied relieved that he didn't say anything more than that about it." "Oh, Bryant," he said. "What did you make on your ACT?" Ashamed of my score, I reluctantly said, "I made a sixteen. It was after a game. I am taking it again in December after the season." "All right, what is your GPA, because if it is high enough you will be fine?" "I have a 3.69, and, yes, I know, Coach, but my pride will not let me settle for a sixteen. I'm taking it again." "I hear ya, buddy," he said. "Great mind-set. Hey, the Sun Herald called me and wants to do a feature on you in the sports section. They want to know when the best day would be to call you?" "They can call on a Wednesday or Thursday," I said. "All right, I will let them know," he said. "Now I don't know when they will call or put it in the paper." "OK, Coach," I said. That conversation made me feel better about the whole thing and canceled my worries. "No man can close a door that I have opened," I said out loud to myself, referring to Revelations chapter three verse eight from the Bible. "Thank you, Lord," I looked up at the ceiling in reverence to Him.

I could now focus on getting healthy and finishing my senior season. When Monday came, my ankle felt better in all the movements. That morning I walked into the training room for treatment and Mr. Tabb had a grin on his face. "Why are you smiling so hard?" I asked. He went into his office and came back out and said, "Wear this brace and see how you like it. Friday you will most likely wear the one I already gave you because it is better to wear during activities. This brace is to stabilize your ankle as much as possible without adding stress to it. This week we are going to push your ankle a little harder than normal." I just smiled, because he was onboard with me playing that week. I knew I would not be able to play the whole game, but if I could just play a half or a quarter, I would be good. I wanted to play to encourage others, and, of course, I mean, it was Harrison Central. The last time I would take part in playing our high school rivals. I would get to practice with the team a little bit, and I was so excited. It would be limited action but it did not matter. I was back on the field, playing with my teammates. Before I knew it, it was game day, and I was in the training room getting taped. The only people who knew I was going to play were my teammates and coaches. The newspaper had said I was still out with an ankle injury. We started the warm up, and my adrenaline was pumping, so I couldn't feel my ankle hurting that much. That was before I took something for the pain.

When we broke it down we went to routes on air. On the left side of the field I could do everything vertical and breaking in. I knew I couldn't do anything breaking out because it was too much pressure on my right ankle. As we got to the out route, Coach called me up, "Bryant, you can't do any routes breaking out can you?" "No," I said, "not really. I mean, I can if I have to, but it hurts super bad, Coach." "Yeah," he said, "that's what I thought. I will keep you vertical or breaking in then." I got back in line to finish routes on air. When we headed inside, Mr. Tabb called me over, "Bryant, how does it feel?" I said, "It burns with a little pain but nothing crazy." "OK," he said, "if it starts hurting or I see you limping, I will pull you." I nodded in agreement. I got into the locker room and went straight to my boy Bernard so I could get some Ibuprofen. "Bryant, are you all right, Cuz?" he said. I stared at Bernard as he handed me the pills and said, "Yeah, bra. I'm good." "If you are good," he said, "why are you taking these? Why did you ask me for them?" "Because, bra," I said, "the pills will allow me to play for a half." Bernard shook his head and said, "No, Bryant." He went to tell Coach, but I grabbed his arm and said, "Come on, bra, let me play." He said, "It ain't worth it, B. You have a full scholarship. You going to school for free. Why would you jeopardize that?" "Because," I said, "I can't explain it. When I can't play . . . Man, I don't know." "Naw, B," he said, "I'm not letting you play." "For my Dad," I said. "Let me play a half for my Dad. Just a half. I promise." "A'ight," he said, "for him, B. I'm pulling you out if I see you limping." I nodded my head in agreement. Coach Banks came up to me and said, "Bryant, how do you feel?" I said, "I'm eighty-five percent, Coach." "Are you good enough to go?" "Yes, sir!" I said. He nodded and walked away. Bernard was right, but I wanted to play. God had me so I was good.

We broke it down and headed onto the field. I always got in the back of the line during the run out. The front of the line was for the hyped people. I never got hyped during pre-game. I was the calm guy for the most part, other than when I gave speeches. When we ran out of the tunnel, I was the last person out, and I heard an eruption from the crowd. It was amazing to feel the love from fans. When the game started, Coach gave me a hitch to open the game up, which was great for me to get everything rolling because as the game went on it was a tight one. At that time of the year we were running the ball more so I had to make the most of every ball that came my way. Coach called a time out. "Bryant, can you run a post corner?" "Yes, just let me run it to the left," I said. "Do you think he will be able to get it to you?" he said. "Coach, as long as he gets it in my vicinity I will catch it," I said. "The DB can't hold me. I will be wide open." "OK, Bryant," Coach said before calling the play for the offense in the huddle. We broke and ran to the field. As I lined up, I looked at how much room I had and where the DB was lined up. He was in off-man, slightly inside.

The ball was hiked and I came off hard and stuck to the post; on my third step, stuck to the corner. Just as I had said, I was wide open. The quarterback overthrew me, I dove for the ball, and it was still too far. It went straight out of bounds. I stayed on the ground for an extended period, because that was the last play of that game for me. That route took everything out of my ankle for the game. I got off the ground and jogged to the locker room with my teammates. I went to Mr. Tabb when I saw him and said, "I can't go anymore." He gave me a nod. Bernard walked over and said, "Yo, B, are you straight?"

"Yeah, bra," I replied, "y'all just have to finish getting this W without me, bra." He nodded and said, "Bro, we got you. You just do what you have to do right now. You are going to the next level." Coach Banks walked over and said, "Bryant, can you go?" I just shook my head, no. He walked away and went to address the team. I took off my shoulder pads and put my jersey back on as everyone started to head to the field.

When we got out there I found John and hung with him to discuss what was going on with the game. The coaches asked us what we saw, and we gave them detailed answers based on the questions they asked. The game stayed tight throughout the second half and eventually came down to an extra point. If the Rebels make the kick, we would go into overtime. If they missed, we would win. I got on my knees and said, "Please miss, please miss, please miss." The ball was snapped, kicked, and it went wide left. Everyone rushed the field. We had just beaten our rival.

The next week would be the last game of our season and the last game of my senior year. We would be playing our Coast rival Biloxi Indians. Unfortunately, we would not go to the playoffs but we could finish 6-4 with wins over both rivals. The year before we had lost to both of them, but this year we had an edge and a better chance to come out 2-0 against our rivals. The whole week's practice had an emphasis on the run game. I knew we would not throw the ball at all. During the game that Friday I really just ran routes to play games with the defensive backs. I also let some of the young receivers get in the game. We rotated every series, because the game was boring, for one because we were not throwing the ball at all, and two, we were blowing Biloxi out. The clock hit zero, and it finally hit me that I would never again put on a football jersey for Gulfport High school. A tear fell down my face, because I had accomplished one step toward a major goal I had for my life, and the next time I put on a football jersey it would be to represent the University of South Alabama.

Questions

1. Have you matched your work with your faith?
2. Do you try to control the outcome when you notice the small cuts?
3. Do you stay humble when you get a breakthrough?

CHAPTER 6

New Creature:
Transformed Mind

RECRUITING PROCESS

Just like I had told Coach Dean I would do, shortly after the season was over I took the ACT again. I just had to wait on my results. I also got the phone call from the newspaper. Below is a bit of the story that resulted from that interview:

Gulfport wide receiver Bryant Lavender always dreamed of playing college football near his Gulfport hometown.

South Alabama will accommodate him next year. The All-South Mississippi performer has verbally committed to play for the Jaguars inaugural team next season. He will sign a national letter of intent Feb. 1, National Signing Day. Lavender is ranked seventh among South Mississippi seniors selected by the Sun Herald.

"My mother didn't want me to go off far away to college," Lavender said. "Now I can come home anytime I want to." South Alabama will play exhibition games next season before eventually becoming a Division 1 team in five years as a member of the Sun Belt Conference.

"The South Alabama coaches were very enthusiastic toward me," Lavender said. "They showed me a lot of love and were down to earth." Lavender, 6-foot-1, caught the eye of Jim Doon, who covers Mississippi recruiting for Scout.com, at a New Orleans camp this spring.

"Bryant showed out for us at our combine in New Orleans," Doon said. "He made the all-combine team and was the consensus pick as the top receiver in attendance. He needs to add bulk, but he has some nice upside."

Lavender is a solid student who has already qualified academically to play as a true freshman next season. He has a 3.4 GPA and is trying to increase his ACT score. "It's very important for me to play college football," Lavender said. "I can get a good education, good job and help the young kids out. I want to major in physical education and become a coach. That way, I can teach the young kids."

South Alabama projects Lavender as a wide receiver, but he could also play defensive back. He's a dual performer for the Admirals. "They have me playing receiver, but if they want to move me, that's fine," Lavender said. "I'll play where ever they want." Returning kicks is a hidden aspect of Lavender's game. He's considered one of the Coast's top game-breaking threats.

"I always want the ball in my hands because I can make plays," Lavender said. "I have a knack for making the big play. My work ethic and always wanting to get better make me a good player." Lavender's desire to excel is what impresses Gulfport coach Don Banks, who has coached his share of major college recruits at Madison Central.

"Bryant is a good all-around athlete," Banks said. "He's a good receiver, a good leader, team player, captain and a leader.

The day after that was in the Sports section, I got to school and everyone was congratulating me with high-fives, and pats on the back. There was so much love from everyone at my high school and I saw it as a chance to prove everyone who counted me out wrong. I got to homeroom, and I asked if I could go see Coach Hood. I pulled the Sports section out of one of the copies of newspapers I had. I didn't see her standing outside the door, so I walked into her class and she said, "Bryant what are you doing?" "I have something I want you to read," I said. "What is it?" she said, so I tossed the Sports section onto her desk and walked out with a grin on my face. The whole time I was thinking, "Talking about I was not going to get a scholarship. Don't ever doubt me." Later on that day I saw Coach Hood at the basketball game. I smiled and giggled. She giggled and said, "OK, South Alabama, I ain't mad at you." Finally, no one could say anything about what took place, because God made everyone be quiet by the way he blessed me with that scholarship. Everything God had taken me through until that point was preparing me for that moment. All I could do was thank Him.

The next week I checked on the score for my ACT and saw that I made the eighteen I needed to fully qualify. "Thank you, Lord! Jesus, thank you!" I exclaimed as I stood up out of the chair and did a little dance in the computer room. Later that week Coach Dean came to visit me. He, Coach Coe and I sat down and had a great conversation. We sat in the courtyard where students eat lunch. "Coach Dean, I made an eighteen on the ACT," I said. "I sent the scores straight to the school." "Good deal, Bryant," he said. "I will get it when I get back to school." That was really all I was worried about so I did not have to take any remedial classes once I got to South. Coach Dean looked at me and asked, "Bryant, do you know the details of the scholarship that we have given you?" I replied, "Well, Coach, I know that if you get redshirted that you get an extra year. Also, if you get hurt that you get a medical redshirt and also get another year. Coach, I want to be a true freshman. I don't want to be redshirted." He looked at me with a straight face and said, "Bryant, I'm going to be honest with you. It is very rare for a freshman to come in and play right away. True freshman means that you are outright better than everyone they have already at your position. You have to know the playbook like the back of your hand in a matter of months, literally, and gain the coach's trust that you know what to do on every play. Not saying that you are not able to do that. I am saying that is the coach's thinking before he decides to play a true freshman. You get five years to play four, in that time you can get a degree and start your master's. You will have a solid year to get bigger, stronger, faster and have the system engrained in your brain. All you have to do is show progress to renew." I interrupted, "Renew?" "Your scholarship," he said.

My facial expression showed confusion and I said, "Coach, I thought when you sign you are there for those four or five years unless you decide to transfer." "No sir," he said, "you are signing a one-year contract. What you did on the high school level is what got you the scholarship. Now what you do while you are at the school you signed to will keep you there. Basically, what I am saying, you can get cut from the team. If the coaches do not think you are reaching the potential they thought you would have, they will not renew your scholarship. They are one-year contracts. Nobody is going to waste money on someone who is not reaching his or her potential. Once you get to school you are fighting every day, fighting to keep your spot, fighting to stay eligible and fighting to stay on scholarship." I just sat there downloading that new information. Still shocked by all of what he had just said.

Then he hit me with more information, "Bryant, have you ever heard of a grey shirt?" I scrunched my face up and said, "No, sir. What is that?" He said, "That is when a program signs too many players in a year, so they have to use the next year's scholarships granted that they do not have NCAA violations. So, you sign with the class you came out with, but will not technically come to school until the next year's class." "Oh, OK," I said. That conversation had just blown my mind. There was so much about going to college as an athlete that I did not know.

We moved on to the next topic of discussion, which was when would I want to make my visit to the school. I had a choice between senior bowl weekend or the weekend after. Honestly, I did not care about going to the senior bowl because that would be the focal point of the visit. I wanted to see the school, and what type of environment I would be dealing with on a regular basis. I told him I would go the week after but he said he would give me a call the next week to confirm my decision.

Another thing I was surprised about was that Coach Coe didn't have much to say about what Coach Dean had told me. I'm sure he knew most of what was talked about, but he allowed me to take in the information from someone else. He was like my physical guardian angel in this athletic world. He was there so I wouldn't be lied to, so I would feel comfortable when all that information was thrown at me. He was there to break down things that I did not fully understand. Coach Dean was a friend to Coach Coe. I saw that both of them had a sense of trust and respect for one another.

CHANGES

Coach Dean called me just as we were about to get out for Christmas break. He told me my official visit would be January 17, 2009. He asked to speak to my mother, so I went into the den and said, "Mama, Coach Dean wants to talk to you." I handed her the phone and put it on speaker. "Hey, Coach. How are you?" she said. "I'm great, Mrs. Lorna. How are you?" he replied. "I'm marvelous, honey!" she said, and they both laughed at her reply. "Mrs. Lorna," he said, "I wanted to know if you wanted to come with Bryant on his visit in January." "Yes," she said. "You know I want to come. That is my son, correct?" Coach Dean laughed before answering, "Yes, ma'am. He is all yours. We just have to ask. How many people are coming? Do you want to drive? Or do you want us to pick you up?" "It is going to be three of us," she said, "and we are going to drive. How far is Mobile from Gulfport?" Coach replied, "Oh, it is only about an hour east of where you are now." "OK," Mom said. "Yeah, we are going to drive." "All right," Coach said. "I will put you all down on the list with the other recruits coming in that day. If I do not talk to you all before -- Merry Christmas and Happy New Year."

Two days away from Christmas, Mississippi Gulf Coast Community College's Coach Feeney called me and said, "Hey, Bryant, how are you?" "I'm great, Coach" I said. "How are you?" "I am fine," he said. "I want to know if you are ready to be a Bulldog." "Um, Coach, I'm going to South." He immediately hung up the phone. I just laughed to myself. I was not expecting him to just hang up in my face.

Shortly after I started back watching TV, I got a call from Coach Lute. "Hey, Bryant, how are you doing, big'n'?" he said. "Merry Christmas to you and your family." I said, "I am doing great, Coach. Merry Christmas to your family as well." "Thank you, Bryant," he said. "I really appreciate that; let me get down to business. Are you going to come be a Lion or what? I know you have an offer from South Alabama, but you are better than them. They don't think you are that good of a player anyway. I've talked to them. Listen, you can come here for a semester and leave in December and go to the university of your choice. All twenty-two of our starters signed to Division 1 schools. No other JUCO in the country can say that." "Coach," I said, "that is impressive, I have to say. I have already committed to South." "That's fine and good," he said, "but they are not going to use you like they should. They do not know what type of player you are. I do. Why don't you just come be a Lion?" "Coach," I said, "it is a dream of mine to go straight to a university out of high school. Coach, I am going to South." "OK, Bryant," he said, "when they mess you over. You will come calling, and I will have a scholarship waiting on you." Click. He hung up the phone. I couldn't believe that he got mad at me for following my dreams. Oh well, God told me to go here, so I know everything will work out like it should.

The day after Christmas I received a text message from Coach Dean. I smiled, because

I anticipated the good news he would always bring when we spoke. It read:

"Hey, Bryant. Coach Dean here. Just wanted to let you know that I have taken the offensive coordinator position at Mississippi State University. I will no longer be in contact with you. I have given all of your recruiting material to Coach Charo. He is the tight-end coach and will finish out your recruiting process."

My stomach dropped after reading that message. I couldn't believe that I was already having a coaching change and I was not at school yet. My reply:

"Wait. So you will not be at South anymore?"

I sent that back, because I was shocked at what I had read, I wanted to make sure that my eyes were not playing tricks on me.

Coach Dean: "No, Bryant. I will not be there. I am sorry. Coach Charo will be there and handle everything for you."

Me: "Coach Charo? I don't know him. He will not treat me the same. I'm your recruit."

Coach Dean: "I know Bryant. I am sorry for putting you into this spot, but I promise you the staff at South Alabama will take care of you."

Me: "Okay Coach. Thank you for everything"

That was it. Coach Dean was in my life and out just like that. I trusted him. I didn't know if I would or could trust anyone else on the staff, but hopefully this Coach Charo was an all right dude. I had to call Coach Coe and inform him of the news, so I called him and said, "Hey, Coach!" He cut me off, and said, "Hey, Bryant, I just got the news. How do you feel?" "Well," I said, "I just wish he would have called me instead of texting me. Other than that, I am OK. Do you know this Coach Charo?" "Charo?" he replied, "Yeah, I know him." I said, "How do you feel about him, because he is the one that will finish my recruiting process?" Coach Coe said, "To be honest, Bryant, I really do not care for him too much." Great! That was not what I wanted to hear because if Coach Coe didn't like the guy, chances were, I wouldn't either. "Dang! All right," I replied to his statement. I got off the phone with Coach and started talking to God, "Lord God, please let all of this finish out smoothly. You told me to come to South. Please give me the strength to deal with what just happened. Lord, I am leaving everything in your hands. Amen!"

The first day back at school I got called to Coach Coe's office. When I walked into his office I saw this other guy in his office. "Bryant, how are you? I am Coach Charo," he said with a Cajun accent. "Hey, Coach, how are you," I said not really paying attention to anything else he was saying. I just analyzed his body language. I came to the conclusion that I was not too fond of him. After the meeting was over, I just thought about what Coach Coe said to me in the previous conversation about him. He just did not stack up well compared to Coach Dean. I hoped that when I went on my visit I would get a better vibe. So many thoughts came to my mind wondering if it would be anything like I had already seen. Are the players really good? Will I play? Will I meet my best friends like my Mom said I would? How different would it be when I get there?

That day when I got home I had a package waiting for me on the table. It had a USA seal on it, and when I picked it up it had some weight to it. When I opened it, I pulled out the spiral-bound book that read, "Spring Workout 2009." As I opened it, I saw it had tabs for "Nutrition," "Warm-ups," "Technique" and "Workout." I pulled out another sheet of paper from the package and it read, "2009 Commits." Along with it was a DVD to watch. It had all the commits on it with a few highlight clips from the season. After I watched the highlights from the other receivers I thought, "Oh, dang! They good. You better get ready or you will not play."

Up until that moment I had planned on not running track my last year of high school. I had been ducking Coach Carter and Coach Pee since we had gotten back to school. After seeing those boys on the film, I decided I needed to be in shape. I went to practice the next day. "Oh, Bryant. How nice of you to join us. I thought you weren't going to run," Coach Carter said. I smiled and said, "Well, Coach, I've had a change of heart." "I don't know why your butt was playing like you were not going to run," Coach Pee said. "You have to be in some kind of shape before you go to college." I laughed and said, "Yeah, I realized that." They both shook their heads at me, but I knew I had to get right before I left or I would be well behind the pack once I got to school.

Two weeks flew by and as soon as my parents were off work we headed to Mobile, Alabama, for my official visit. We were meeting at the Battle House Hotel in downtown Mobile. When we pulled up to the hotel, I had never seen one like that before in person. We walked in, and it was like something you would see in a movie. We checked in, got our room numbers, and they told us to come back down because we would be going to eat soon. We found the elevators and figured out which floors we were on. My parents were on a separate floor, and they got off of the elevator before me and I got off a few floors later. When I got to my room, it was decked out in red, white and blue. There was a cookie cake with my name on it along with an itinerary for the weekend. I just glanced at the paper, stuck it in my pocket and rushed downstairs to look at the tables that were set up with possible jersey combinations.

Five minutes later, they instructed everyone to go downstairs to get on the little buses formally known as Jagtrans. They also let us know that was what we would be using to go to classes during the fall and spring semesters. As we were driving through the city, the guide was telling us about the city, but all I was doing was looking at everyone and taking the whole experience in. I didn't really care what the guide was saying at that point. We pulled up at a restaurant called Wintzell's. Had never heard of them before but from what the coaches were saying it was supposed to be one of the best seafood spots in the city. The Jagtrans came to a stop, and we fell out of them one by one. When we entered the restaurant, we were escorted straight to the back. My host for the weekend was waiting for us in the back room. The hosts were responsible for visitors like me when we were out of sight of the parents and coaches on the visit. As I crossed the threshold of the door to the backroom there was a guy with short, red hair and freckles looking directly at me. He said, "Bryant?" I nodded my head yes. "Hey, man, I am Tyler Wells," he said. "I will be your host for the weekend." I shook his hand, and he showed me where my seat was. "How was your drive down?" "It was good," I said. "It honestly was just a straight shot from where I live." "Good," he said. "I looked up your city, and it said it was only an hour away." "Yep, so it wasn't a bad drive at all," I replied. "Did you have any other schools looking at you?" "Yeah," I replied, "East Mississippi and Mississippi Gulf Coast, but I always wanted to go straight to a university. South is a university and made the best offer, as well as feeling like one big family. That's why I committed." "Cool," he said. "Yeah, man, that is definitely one of the key reasons I chose this place as well." "Do you play receiver also?" I said. "Yeah, I do," he said. I nodded my head in agreement with what he had said while also acknowledging that he would be my competition. "Where are you from?" I asked. "I am from Niceville, Florida," he said. "That is about two and half hours away from here." "Oh, OK. Cool. What would you say your best attribute as a receiver is?" I asked that question only because I felt Tyler would be upfront with me. He looked at me with a bit of a surprised expression, but I saw he thought about what I had asked him. "Well," he said, "I would say catching the ball, because I'm not super-fast, and I do not make many people miss, but I normally catch everything thrown in my direction." "Possession," I said, "I like that. I mean, that is what you are here for; to catch the ball." We both laughed a little bit after I made that statement. My Mom interjected and began to talk to Tyler for a while. I just began to scan the room, looking at my future teammates. I could not believe I was in a place I had dreamed of when I was younger.

Right before the food was brought to us, Coach Stone had a few words to say, "Welcome everyone. We are glad everyone could make it here safely, and we want you to know that this is a major step for this program. You all are taking part in history in the making. Thank you to everyone who took part in setting up for this great weekend, and to the recruits and your families who are here: Welcome to the Jag family! The food will be out shortly. After everyone eats, the recruits will be free to leave with their designated hosts, and parents will go back to the hotel. Hosts, do not have them out too late; we have a long day tomorrow. Thank you again and Go Jags!" After Tyler and I got done eating, we left the restaurant. He wanted to show me the campus and where I would be living when I got on campus. When we got in his car and headed toward the school Tyler was giving me information about the city, like what streets are good to take, where good places are to hang out with friends and things to do on campus. The last thing he spoke about was the Fellowship of Christian Athletes, also known as FCA. That is what grabbed my attention because I had planned on getting involved with that organization. What better way to be connected to it? Not only was Tyler a member of the organization, but he also was the president of the organization. That's when I knew God was totally in control because He gave me a believer for a host.

Tyler broke down the whole campus when we reached the school. We went through the main entrance of the school. He drove slowly and broke down every building for me and where I would possibly have classes in each building. He showed me where the café, student center and bookstore were. They were all connected in one huge building at that time. As we get deeper into campus he showed me where the dorms were, there were only four Gamma, Beta, Epsilon and Delta. He told me that I would most likely be in Delta 1. "Bryant, you know what co-ed dorms mean?" Tyler asked. "Yeah, that is where girls and boys are in the same dorm." I said. "That is right," he said. When he told me that, I was a bit surprised because all the other stories of college said there were just all-boys or all-girls dorms. The Delta dorms, he explained, were mostly freshmen dorms, but not limited only to freshmen. He explained how a lot of the upperclassmen went to Beta, Gamma or Grove Apartments. When we pulled up to the Grove, I was amazed because it was a real apartment complex. He was trying to explain how the buildings were numbered, but it was so confusing I really didn't pay any attention to it. Tyler parked the car, and we walked into a room, and there were about seven people in there. He introduced me to all of them. I was just looking at everything, how the room was set up, the way everyone had a laid-back vibe, the way they were so open to talk to me and how they asked me questions. After that I just watched how they interacted with one another. I literally just watched them for an hour. Tyler asked me if I was ready to go back to the hotel, and I said yes. It had been a long day and I had begun to get tired. Going back to the hotel seemed shorter than it had when we were leaving the hotel to go to campus. As soon as I got back, I went to my parents' room. When I opened the door, my stepfather and mother were in robes looking bougie, "Hey, son. How was your evening?" my stepfather asked. "It was cool," I said. "We went to the campus, saw some buildings. I met some more football players and a few other athletes at the apartments called the Grove." "Did you have fun?" my Mom asked. "Yes, Ma'am," I said. "What have y'all been doing?" "You see us don't you," she said. "We living like a king and queen right now." We let out a huge laugh. We talked for a few more minutes before I went back to my room.

The next morning, we ate breakfast at huge round tables and the coaches sat with different people than they had sat with the night before. Coach Stone actually visited every table before we finished up our breakfast, and we left to do the school tour. Our school tour showed us around campus but most of the places Tyler had already showed me the night before, so I felt a little ahead of everyone else. Only difference was I could see the buildings clearly because it was daylight. We stopped at the student center because that is where our lectures would take place about the school and possible majors to go into, and where the bookstore was so we could buy apparel. "Bryant, do you want to go into the store?" my Mom asked. "No Ma'am," I said. "I will see it enough when I get here. I am ready to hear about the majors." "Me, too, baby," she said. "You know what you want to major in?' "Kind of," I said, "but they don't have all the majors represented today. So, I think I will go to physical education." My Mom just nodded. They gathered us up and broke us into groups based on the interest of major.

They escorted us into the classrooms in the back of the student center. I really wanted to hear about the physical therapy program, because that's what I wanted to major in, but because it wasn't represented I had to go to the closest thing. I went into the physical education room, and it was the biggest group. As the representative started to explain and go into detail about the major she would stop to see if we had questions. I would ask something every time. Everyone would look at me with curious faces to see what I would ask next. We spent about an hour and a half in the classroom and when we finished they gave us ten minutes to use the bathroom. I didn't have to use the bathroom, so I went to look at the amphitheater and to look at the campus from behind the student center. The mother of one of the recruits was out there as well. "Hey, how are you?" I asked, she smiled back and replied, "I'm great." As she began to walk away she stopped and said, "You must make straight A's in school." I had a confused smile on my face, "No, ma'am not all A's. Why do you ask that?" "Because of all the questions you were asking," she said. "Very detailed." I chuckled a little while a big smile formed on my face, "This is the school I will possibly spend the next four to five years at," I said. "I just wanted to confirm some things that I have read." She said, "Do you go to a white school? You speak so well." "No, ma'am. Actually I go to a school that is fifty percent down the middle between white and black. My Mom makes my brothers and me speak correctly. If we don't, we will get in trouble." She smiled and said, "She did an amazing job." I smiled back and said, "Thank you."

Everyone was loading back on the Jagtrans. It was time to go see where the football complex was being built. As we went up the hill, there was a foundation, bricks and support beam poles. Coach Stone stood before us. He was wearing a beige pea coat and boots and said, "Everyone, follow me. I will show you where everything will be. Right here where we are standing will be the entrance. To your right will be the coaches' offices. To your left will be a few offices along with the game room for the players. Everyone take a few steps with me. In this area will be the training room. Two big Jacuzzis; one will be a hot tub and the other is a cold tub. In this part of the training area, there will be twelve training tables. Across the hall will be a weight room the size of a football field. Back behind the training room is the locker room." The equipment workers had put a locker in that area to show us what it would look like. "Here are the lockers and what they will look like. There is a cubby with a lock for valuables. Shoulder pad hangar with a fan so it can air out. The seat lifts up and you put your cleats down here, so they won't be out and there is a fan down here, too, so they can air out as well. Now I am going to show you where we will be practicing." Coach Stone took us behind where the foundation was laid for the complex and up the hill. "Here is where we will practice. There will be two fields. On the right will be the turf field, and on the left will be the grass field." As those words rolled out of Coach Stone's mouth, I could visualize every bit of it. I knew then that I would enjoy my time at South Alabama. After that, we were told that we would go back to the hotel to rest and that we would get back together later for dinner.

When I woke up from my nap I looked at the clock and had fifteen minutes to get downstairs for dinner. When I got downstairs, I ran into another recruit who was wearing a black V-neck, some Levi's jeans and shell-toe Adidas. When he noticed me, he reached out his hand and said, "What's up, bra? My name is Vernel Champ. I am a running back from Hillcrest High School from Tuscaloosa, Alabama." "What's up, bra? I am Bryant Lavender, receiver from Gulfport High School from Gulfport, Mississippi," I said while shaking his hand back without hesitation. "Gulfport, is that like right by Biloxi?" "Yeah," I said, "it is actually the next city over." "Oh, for real," he said, "so is it closer to Mobile or further?" "Just a little further," I said. "It goes Moss Point, Gautier, Ocean Springs, Biloxi and then Gulfport." "OK, cool," he said. "So, was South the only school you had looking at you?" "No," I said. "I had some JUCO offers, but I didn't want to go to them." "Which ones offered you?" he asked. "I had Mississippi Gulf Coast and East Mississippi," I replied. "Oh, I have heard of them," he said. "They've had pretty good teams for the last few years." "Yeah," I said, "they both do." "Why don't you want to go to them?" he said. "Well, I made a promise to myself that I wanted to go straight to a university out of high school," I said. "Word. I feel that," he said. When Vernel and I had finished the conversation, it was time to go to dinner. We pulled up to Slap Jacks, and I saw my host, Tyler. Today they had the hosts and recruits sitting together, so we could meet each other. We found out that there was a party going on. It was frat party. I tapped Vernel, "Aye, bra," I said. "You going to the frat party?" "Yeah, bra," he said. "I gotta check it out. I gotta see what the hype is about." I laughed and said, "I was thinking the same thing." We dapped each other up to confirm that we were going to the party. I looked at Tyler and said, "Are we going to the frat party everyone is talking about?" "Sure man," he said, "whatever you want to do. I may have to ask one of the other hosts to take you back to the hotel, because I have church in the morning." "All good, bro. I'll just ride with Vernel and his host," I told Tyler. "OK, sounds great, Bryant."

I couldn't lie, I was excited to see what this frat party was about. We left the restaurant and went to the hotel to change before going to the party. I went up the stairs changed into my black sweater came back down, hopped into Tyler's car and we headed toward the party. When we pulled up to the house where the party was being held, it was packed. There were cars everywhere. After we got into the party the first thing I did was look for Vernel, but he had not made it yet. There were other people from the football team at the party. Tyler took me over to introduce me to them. Along the way, we found a spot to stand in the process. I just looked at everything that was transpiring; I had never seen anything like that before – group of young people having a good time with no signs of confrontations. Everyone was just having a great time. While I was taking in the atmosphere, I felt a tap on my shoulder. It was Vernel, "What's up, bra!" I dapped him up and said, "What's good, bra!" We both turned to look at the people enjoying the atmosphere of the party. One of the players came up to us said, "Aye, these females are not just going to come dance with y'all. You better go get them!" Vernel and I just looked at each other without moving. "Oh y'all think I'm playing, huh?" he said. "Don't worry about it. I got you." "Naw, bra, I can do it myself," I said, speaking up for myself. "All right, freshmen," he said. "Show me something then." He stepped back to watch me make a move. I scanned the room to see what area I wanted to go to. I felt Vernel hit my arm, "Go 'head, bra." He said with a laugh. I walked to the right corner of the room and saw a young lady in a navy-blue dress. I walked up to her and whispered in her ear, "Would you like to dance?" She turned and looked me in my face, gave me a quick scan before nodding yes. As she started dancing with me, I began to ask questions. "Do you go to South?" "No, I got to Spring Hill," she responded. "What year are you?" "I am a junior," she said. "What about you?" "I am a freshman, at South," I said. "You little baby!" she said. "But yet here you dancing with the baby," I said while giving her a funny face. We both giggled at my responses. We danced for about five songs straight and then she grabbed me closed and whispered in my ear, "I leaving. I have a kickback to go to. Thank you for the dance." "No, thank you," I replied. We hugged and as she left, she grabbed my hand and let go while she walked away. I watched her disappear into the darkness. When I went back to stand by Vernel all he said was, "Dog, you were over there dancing with her for a minute." "Bra, I know," I said. "So, bra," he said, "I know you got her number." I just dropped my head and shook my head no, "I forgot to ask." "No! B," he said, "you have to lock them in before they leave. You will never see her again, bro. It's over with." I couldn't do anything but laugh.

We got back to the hotel at three o'clock in the morning and had to have breakfast at eight in the morning. I woke up a seven thirty packed my bags, and went down to eat breakfast. I was tired because it had been a long night. As soon as I got to the table my Mama said, "Bryant you look sleepy." "I am," I said while smashing the breakfast that was in front of me. She laughed and didn't say anything else. Coach Stone stood up after finishing his food and said, "Good morning, everyone. I just want to thank you all for coming to the University of South Alabama. Thank you for allowing us to show you what we have to offer your sons through education as well as football. To the commitments, we got this weekend, Welcome to the jungle. To the ones who are undecided, come be a part of history. I hope everyone enjoyed themselves. Please be safe as you travel to your homes. God bless." That officially concluded my visit to the University of South Alabama. We said our goodbyes, and I told Vernel I would see him soon. He told me that he would hit me up on Facebook. My parents and I got on the road and I had them drop me off at church when we got back to Gulfport.

A few weeks later, I received priority mail. "Mama," I said, "you know what this is?" As I looked at it, I saw that it was from USA. "No, baby," she said, "I think it is from South." "Yeah, I see," I said. "Well it has to be important because it is priority mail." As I walked on the other side of the bed we opened the mail and out fell two sheets of yellow paper. I read the top. It was the letter of intent to go to school. "Mama," I said, "when I sign this, they get to tell me what to do. I'm about sign my life over." She laughed and said, "Go 'head baby."

They gave me two of the same papers. So, I signed one in front of my Mom. The other I was going to sign on the actual day of February fourth. My school told me to bring my letter of intent on the fourth. They wanted to take pictures and the newspaper as well as the news station would be there. That Friday morning they called me and Jerry Williams to the library. We were the only two guys at my school who were going to play football in college. As we took photos I couldn't believe that moment was happening. The only thing I really disliked was that Coach Banks got in my picture when he didn't coach me for real. Coach Coe should have been in the picture because he was the one who impacted me the most. "Yo, Bryant, you know my brother Johnny is going over there to South," Jimmy said. "No, I didn't but that's great. I will have some family there," I replied to him. "That's right," he said. A few hours later I get a call to come to the office. When I walked into the office I saw Tyler and his roommate. "Hey, guys, what are you doing here?" I said. "Hey, man," Tyler said, "we came to watch you sign your letter of intent." "For real?" I said. "You missed it. I signed at 9 a.m. Thank you for coming, though. I really appreciate it." "Well why don't you give us a tour of your school?" Tyler said. The principal gave me the OK to show them around.

Everything was going according to plan, or so I thought, until I received a phone call from Coach Geno one afternoon. I answered the phone, "Hello." "Bryant, what's up? Do you have time to talk right now?" "Yeah, coach," I said. "Everything OK?" At the same time, I mouthed to my weight room teacher that it was South on the phone. So, he allowed me to step outside. "OK," Coach Gene said. "Well, I have some news for you. We just got out of a staff meeting, and we want to grey shirt you. Do you know what that is?" My heart dropped, I scrunched up my face, "I have heard of it, yes," I said. "But can you tell me what that exactly means, please?" "Basically," he said, "we gave out too many scholarships this year and as a coaching staff we feel that you are not as polished as some of the other guys who are coming in. So, we want to grey shirt you and what will happen is, instead of you coming in the summer or fall you will come in during the spring." "OK," I said, "so I signed with my class and technically come in with the next class?" "Yes, that is correct," he responded. "So, coach," I said, "what am I supposed to do until then?" "Well, you can work, stack up some paper or you can enroll in school and start taking classes," he said. "No, Coach," I said, "I can't stay here and work. If I come to school I would have to pay for it until I get on scholarship to be pulled up?" "Bryant," he said, "give me ten minutes and I'll call you back. After we hung up, I paced back and forth for the whole ten minutes. I could not believe what had just happened. Everything had been going according to plan until that day. "God, there is no way this is happening like this. Did I miss something I was supposed to do?" I asked God right before the phone rang. When I heard the phone ring I immediately answered, "Hey, Coach, what's up?" "OK, Bryant, good news," he said. "Are you willing to come for the summer to put in work?" "Yes, sir," I said without hesitation. "OK," he said, "we can put you on scholarship for the summer. There are a few guys doing this to fight for a spot this fall as well." "Put my name on the list, Coach," I said. "I'm coming." "OK," he said, "see you on the twenty-sixth. Good luck." That had been a strange call, but I had an opportunity to change their plans and to make them honor their original commitment. When I got home, I checked Facebook and saw that I had an unread message from Vernel; he told me that he would room with Tre Donald who was a receiver from the same city. That did not shake me because of the situation that I was in; I completely understood why he would not have chosen me to room with because I did not know if I would be there for the fall. It encouraged me to show everyone that I was worthy. From there out, the plan was to trust God and let Him work out the impossible while I did the possible.

I walked across the stage for my high school diploma on May 20, 2009, and enrolled into the University of South Alabama six days later getting ready to start college and fight for my scholarship to go from grey shirt to traditional. When my family left and shut the door I just looked around in silence, I walked over to my bed and turned the TV on while thinking, "You are here now, and there is no going home." Tears rolled down my face because I knew I was up for a tough obstacle, and I could only depend on God to move on my behalf. I texted Vernel to see when he would get in town. He replied that he would be in tomorrow. We had our first team meeting in the graphics building, which had been deemed the headquarters for the football offices until the football complex would be finished in August. The next day around 10 a.m., I heard a knock on the door. When I opened it Vernel was standing outside. "What up, bra?" he asked. "Nothing," I replied. "Just chilling until we have this meeting. Do you need some help moving in?" "Yeah, bra," he said. "I do. I have a lot of stuff." I threw on some shoes and went down to his room and Tre Donald was there as well. We did not say much at first, because we were busy moving them into their room. When we finished moving everything, we had a chance to talk. "You were number 9 for a red team, right?" I said. "Yeah," he replied, "I went to Central Tuscaloosa, and you are from Florida, right? Gators?" he said. I smiled and said, "No, I'm from Mississippi. The G on the helmet stands for Gulfport Admirals."

"Oh, OK," he said, "who recruited you?" "Dean Kilo," I said, "but he took the job at Mississippi State. Who recruited you all?" Vernel jumped in, "Coach Geno recruited both of us. If Geno would have left I probably would have gone somewhere else." "I feel you," I said. "I didn't have any other universities. I had JUCOs, but I did not want to go to them so here I am. Go Jags!" We all chuckled as we walked out of the room, headed to the meeting.

We walked into a room where the whole team and staff were piled in. We met with the athletic training staff, the strength staff and the coaching staff. We received the workout schedule, but we had to choose the time we wanted to work out. I chose 7 a.m. workouts. I wanted to get mine over with at the beginning of the day. We went into the next room to meet the equipment staff and received our gear for the summer. Next, we went to our position room and there were twenty receivers total in the room. "What' s up, y'all? I'm Coach Geno. You should know who I am by now but if you don't, now you do. Introduce yourself to the group and tell everybody where you are from." Everyone took a second to scan the room before anyone said anything. "I'm Tim Jackson from New Orleans, Louisiana. I hope y'all ready to ball because I am." I just looked at Tim who had the confidence of the big man on campus; he was a big receiver standing at 6-feet, 4-inches tall. I did not pay much attention to anyone else other than Tre, and I already knew Tyler, my host. Once everyone had introduced themselves we had to go wait in the hall for further instructions. Tre and I were talking about the meeting we had had when Vernel walked up, so we talked about his meeting. After that, we just cracked jokes, talking about what we planned to eat once we left. All of a sudden, an upper classmen named Tony Reed walked up, tapped me on my shoulder, "Aye, bra!" he said, "what is your name again?" I remember him because he was one of the players I met on my visit. "Bryant Lavender," I answered. He smiled and mocked the way I had said my name. "Naw, bra," he said. "Do you have a nickname or something? Because Bryant sounds too proper, and Lavender is too long." "Well," I said, "some of my friends back home call me B-Lav." He began to walk away, after taking two steps he turned around, "Naw, bra, scratch that," he said. "Take off the B. You are just Lav from now on." I laughed and nodded to accept the name he had given me. Tony then yelled, "Aye, y'all! This is Lav. Everyone say what up, Lav?" Everyone stopped and said, "What up, Lav?" I just threw my hand up to acknowledge everyone.

The next morning Vernel, Tre and I rode together to weights. We got to the weight room also known as the monkey lab. Coach Benny our head strength and conditioning coach was a short, stocky fella with amazing energy all the time. Coach Ron was the stricter one with a bald head. Coach Mak, the youngest one of them, was the most laid back. All were very passionate about their respective fields. If I could classify them, Coach Benny was the weight room guru, Coach Ron was the core guru and Coach Mak was the sprint mechanic guru. They were all highly intelligent individuals. As we got started in the lab, upperclassmen began to open the garage doors that were in the building. Coach Benny explained that we would be on a density-training program. There would be a target of the body with auxiliaries mixed in. There would be four major lifts and we would always finish with abs. We had twelve sets of five at 75 percent of our maximum, and we would start with cleans. There was a seventy-second turn over with four people in a group and for me it was extremely fast. There was ten minutes of straight abs after doing the four lifts. When we finished all of that, I was sure we were finished with the workout, but no. Coach Benny yelled, "You have ten minutes to get to the intramural fields, freshmen follow the upperclassmen." He dashed out of the monkey lab and everyone took off after him. When we got to the field, we had sprints that lasted just as long as the weight workout did. That was the first time in my life that I had gotten sore before I got back to my room. I took a shower, then went straight to sleep.

I did not wake up until a few hours later when I heard a knock on my door. The lactic acid built up so quickly I fell out of the bed when I tried to move. When I finally reached the door, it was Vernel "Aye, bra," he said. "You want to go get something to eat?" "Heck, yeah!" I said. "Let me put some shoes and a shirt on." "All right, man," he said. "We will be in the car." We went to Zaxby's chicken place, came back and went right back to sleep for the rest of the evening. The next day was even worse than the first day, we focused on upper body and the same thing happened again. I got sore before I made it to my room. I mean everything hurt. When I got out of the shower, I reclined in my bed and pondered why I had wanted to come to the summer session. I left because I wanted to prove that I belonged. I left because I did not want to appear as a liar. I left because I wanted to be the person who followed through. It just did not make sense to me, though, that I would be so sore. Then I directed my question to God, "Lord, why didn't you tell me it would be this tough?" Then I spoke to myself, "Do you really want to play college football? Do you really want to go through this?" I went back to God, "God, am I really supposed to be here? If so, God, why does it feel like I am up against so much?" God answered my question when He brought back the question I asked Him years ago when I had asked Him, "God will You allow me to play football at a university and bring the people I need in my life to make that happen?" As that happened the thought of Him fulfilling my question brought tears to my eyes. "I just didn't know it would be this hard," I said to Him. "God, give me the strength to get through this because on my own I will not make it." In that moment I could feel His arms wrap around me to confirm that He would give me everything I needed. I just had to trust Him. I closed my eyes that night knowing everything would work out for my good, because I had been called according to His purpose.

In the last week of the summer Vernel and Tre kept asking me if I had heard something about my scholarship changing from grey shirt. I told them I would not know until the end of the week. During midweek, Kollen came to me right before the workout began, "Lav," he said, "let me holla at you real quick." "What's good, bra?" I asked. "Aye," he said, "they have you on grey shirt don't they?" "Yeah, bra," I said, "They said I would find out if I get pulled up on Friday." "I think I am going to tell Coach I want to grey shirt," he said. "I am going to tell him to switch us." My eyes lit up; I raised my eyebrows and said, "For real, bra? You would do that?" "Yeah, man," he said. "I want to get my knee right. You know I have a torn meniscus. I do not want to start my career injured. I want to have a fresh start, you know? You are healthy, and you work hard so why not switch? We both win in this situation." God just made the way for my scholarship to change. "Thanks, bra!" I dapped him up as Coach Benny blew the whistle to start the workout.

After my workout session on Friday, my phone rang as I was going upstairs to my room. When I looked down, I saw it was Coach Geno calling, I assumed, to tell me the status of my scholarship. "Hey, Coach," I said, "how you doing?" "Lav," he said, "I have some good news for you. We just got out of our staff meeting, and we decided that you are no longer on grey shirt. You will be coming back for the fall." Upon hearing that, all I could do was smile and I said, "So I have regular scholarship opportunities like everyone else? No restrictions?" Coach Geno laughed at my question. "Yeah, Lav," he said, "you have a normal scholarship. You worked hard this summer. Keep it up." I hung up the phone, jumped up and yelled thanking God because I knew He had made the way. Without Him I would have been going back home. I had a five-minute praise break, and then called my Mom to let her know the great news. When I got off the phone, Vernel and Tre came outside because they had heard me yelling about what had happened. They congratulated me, and we were happy that the wolf pack would be in full effect that fall. A huge weight had been lifted off my shoulders. With God's help, I had conquered my first big obstacle with college football. I knew if it was not for Him I would not have gotten that far. Fall camp was to start August third, and classes would finish on the twenty-seventh of July. We had a few days off before we had to be back. I went home and rested my body for a few days before I would have to push my body to the max again.

TRUE FRESHMAN YEAR

The first day of camp was interesting. We had a "Welcome Team" meeting, then the NCAA compliance officers spoke about rules and violations. They made us sign papers agreeing to the rules and statutes. I scanned the room and looked at all of the teammates I would be playing with that year. I just took it all in. That meeting lasted about two hours, then Coach Stone told us to go home and get some rest because we had to be up early for our first official day of practice the next day. I remember that first day of practice as being fast-paced with a lot of yelling, and everything being done at high-intensity despite the heat index having been 120 degrees. It had been so hot outside that day cleats were melting on the turf, coaches and players passed out from heat exhaustion, and Coach Stone had to end practice early because the head athletic trainer said it was just too hot to continue practicing. I remember taking a knee and looking up to hear him as my whole body was drenched in sweat, my heart was beating fast, my mind was racing and I was thankful that God had allowed me to make it through that day.

That is how my whole freshmen fall went. Everything moved so fast while at the same time I was just trying to catch my breath. I felt like a chicken with my head cut off. I was just following the crowd. The hardest part was not being able to form a strong connection with my position coach, Coach Geno, who was a unique coach like none I had ever had before. He possessed great qualities, including his knowledge of the game, that he was down to earth, and that he understood the struggle. He also had some bad qualities, though, including that he showed favoritism, that he was a hothead and that he would tear a player down. I couldn't trust him, because I didn't know whether he might throw something back in my face. While I was not too fond of him as my position coach, I did think he was cool outside of football. Yeah, weird, I know, but that is the best way I can explain it.

Our wide receiver core was a funny bunch, I mostly kept my mouth shut unless I was asking a question or we were having a serious conversation. If you said anything else, you were liable to be talked about. I did not jump into the janking because I could not dish it back out successfully. They had some funny jokes, though, I had to admit. I would not laugh too hard, though, because I did not want those problems — all the jokesters getting back at you, all at the same time. The joking often happened when we were waiting for our position meeting to start. Coach Geno walked in one day and started writing down names on the board. At that point in camp, we were getting closer to the season. Coach Geno said the names he wrote down were the combinations the coaches wanted to see. He said it did not matter where your name fell, because things could still change. We all knew it was a depth chart. I was hoping to play out wide like in high school, but they felt I would be better in the slot. I felt that I had been holding my own pretty well, but that was not the case. My name was on the eighth line of receivers, and it crushed me. I had never been at the bottom of a depth chart. People that low on the depth chart are treated like bums, disrespected by coaches, players and equipment staff. I could not believe they felt I was that bad. What made it worse was my number was eight; I had a daily reminder of where I was at by my number. That day, practice was different for me; it brought everything into perspective for me. I had to prove to them that they were wrong about me. At practice, we were going over blocking, and I took pride in blocking. I blocked hard for my teammate because when it was my turn I wanted them to block for me. During the blocking drill, many of the receivers were complaining about the drill or just did not take part in it. I saw that as an opportunity to make myself relevant. I went multiple times on purpose to show I was not scared to block. We were the last group going in that period because it had gotten heated between the defensive backs and the receivers. The energy brought the whole team and coaches over to view what was taking place. The offensive coordinator, Coach Rubble started yelling, "Receivers have to block. We need tough guys that will stick their noses in there." He took over the drill and Coach Geno started calling names to go in the drill.

Waiting for my name to be called, I thought, "When I go, I will shut it down." Coach Geno called my name fourth. I jumped up to the line and got set. Coach Rubble blew the whistle, and I attacked the defender. We were about a yard apart. I came to balance and loaded my arms to shoot them at the defender. As he got closer, I fired my hands, engaged him and pumped my feet. He started going to my left so I pumped my feet to the left hard. He began to stumble. I pumped my feet harder until he fell. It turned into a pancake. I jumped up and clapped my hands as Coach blew the whistle. Coach Rubble grabbed me, "What is your name son?" "Lavender, Bryant Lavender," I answered. "Lavender, that was one heck of a block you just made." At that, moment things shifted dramatically for me. That block put me on special teams. For the rest of camp. All I could see was where I was on the depth chart, and I fought hard to make changes there. Even though I finished camp strong, I did not move from the bottom of the depth chart. They gave us a few days off before fall classes started, so I gave Coach Coe a call. I told him how I had finished camp and where I was on the depth chart. He could tell that I was bothered by the outcome. He said, "Bryant, keep working your butt off. Do not give them a reason to write you off. Do not be the problem. Be a solution." Those words confused me even more for some reason. I went to God and asked, "God, why are they playing me like I am a scrub? I know I probably should not be starting, but eighth on the depth chart. I know I am better than that." He did not answer me that night because my heart was angry, and I did not give Him time to answer me. I said my problem to Him and walked out of God's spiritual office. I leaned on my own understanding. I did not lend my ear to hear His voice.

There were only seven games on the football schedule because it was the first year South Alabama ever had a football program. Our games were spread out. Every game was two or three weeks apart making our season end on November 12, 2009. I was very excited to start the season with my new team despite where I stood on the depth chart. During the first practice, after we did routes on air, Coach Kint asked for the scout team receivers. I took two swigs of water and began to head over to the defensive side. "Lav, stay here," Coach Geno said. I stopped immediately in my tracks. He sent everyone that was not in the top two lines over except for me. I was confused as to why he had made me stay. I stayed on the offensive side for about three games. I still was confused because how could I be at the bottom of the depth chart but too good to go to scout team. I only practiced for about forty-five minutes every day. This was the most boring couple of months in my football career. I told my parents, Coach Coe, and my friends not to come to any games. I did not want them to waste money to come watch the game if I was not playing. It was a little selfish, I know, but that is just how I felt about the situation I was in. I was going into a depression because of football. I was not playing, hardly practicing, and the equipment managers just treated me like a scrub. I began to question if I had really heard from God about going there. I was very unhappy at South Alabama. I wanted to transfer until one night I had a conversation with God. "God, why is this happening to me? Why did You tell me to come here? I do not like it here." He put Romans 8:28 in my spirit, and we know that all things work together for good to them that love God, to them who are called according to His purpose, KJV. After I read the scripture I asked God, "What's next?" This time I waited for Him to respond back. He simply said, "Go to work." That comforted me and I began to understand that I needed to control the tangible and leave the intangible to Him.

The next day in practice I pulled Coach Geno aside and said, "Hey, Coach can I go over to scout team today?" "You want to go to scout team?" he said, looking confused. "Yeah, because I don't get any reps with the starters, and I wanted to go over there and get better," I said. "OK," he said, "you can go over there. I do not care." Just like that, I demoted myself in order to get better because they had me in the grey area. I just decided to make it plain. Some of the starters talked about me and said that I was making a mistake, but I did not care because I knew what was at stake. I would get to go against the starting DBs all practice and not just for competition periods. So, now, when they called for the scout team I went over with excitement, because I was reviving my love for the game. Vernel had been going to scout team and Tre was a starter. I would not hang with Tre as much during the practice, but I would get to hang with Vernel. "Lav, what are you doing over here?" Coach Seerih, the defensive coordinator asked. "Well," I said, "I asked to come over here because I was not getting any work over there. I came over here to get work." He smiled and nodded at my answer to his question. I walked over to Vernel and said, "Aye, bra, how is everything run over here?" "Just like Skelly, bra," he said, "just get in a group and we roll rapid fire." "Cool," I replied. That day was not a good day for the DBs, because we were gloving everything the quarterback put in the air. All the defensive coaches started yelling at the receivers to drop the ball. I went over to Coach Seerih and said, "Coach, all due respect, but I am not dropping the ball on purpose. That is not what you all brought me here to do." He did not respond back to me but he understood where I was coming from. Therefore, I continued to catch the ball, and the DBs were getting mad at me because of that. I simply said, "The receivers on the other team will not drop the ball on purpose. They will catch everything. I am going to catch the ball." I continued to catch everything and none of the coaches said anything to me.

For the next three weeks, I just got better and better. My confidence grew in my ability and coming out the mental slump did not seem so hard anymore. The best times in practice at that point were when we had competition periods in front of the whole coaching staff, because that was the only chance when the scout team could show our coaches that we were better than what they thought. During that competition period, the scout team was running plays as the offensive of the opponent. The scout defense ran the defensive scheme of the opponent as well. That period was a rotation so every four plays, we would switch the focus of the side of the ball. That gave all the coaches a chance to evaluate starters and see the scout team players. When it was scout offense's turn to go, Coach Geno yelled, "All right, Lav, show me something." On that play I had a go route, and the defensive call was man-coverage. At the snap of the ball, I beat the defensive back off the line. I got in front of him but he was the fastest person on the team so I only had a step on him for a few seconds. I looked back to track the ball in the air, and I saw him digging to catch up. As the ball reached me, he did, too, so I jumped up and snagged the ball out of the air over him. I gave him that look that said, "Yeah, bra, I just mossed you." Everybody went crazy, but I did not. I just went back to the huddle and finished practice. After we broke it down, Coach Geno called me over and said, "Lav, you are getting better, boy. Where did you pull that catch out from?" "Dang, Coach, I do know how to play football," I said, giving him a confused look. We both laughed, but I knew he was serious. He really did not think I could play. Vernel was leaving the field as I was and said, "Lav, what was Geno talking about?" "Man," I said, "he was asking where I learned how to make plays like that as if I just started playing football." Vernel laughed and said, "Bra, you been gloving the ball since you came to scout." "Yeah, I know. They think I am a scrub, Vernel," I replied in a sarcastic tone. Although we laughed Vernel knew that was how I really felt. I knew this would be the last year they disrespected me like that. I found out that I was traveling to the hotel after the walk through on Thursday. I guess I surprised them. At first, I was excited but then I realized that it was just a slap in the face, because I was not expected to play. The itinerary said we had to return to the field house by 4 p.m. so we could leave for the hotel.

When we went back to the field house, Coach Geno came in and said, "Lav! You traveling. How does it feel?" "It's cool," I replied calmly. I answered like that because I knew he was being sarcastic. Tim interjected, "Coach, Lav knows he happy; trying to act all cool like it's not a big deal. Lav, don't front with your black-tar self!" Everyone laughed at Tim, but I ignored him. He could say what he wanted, because he was the big man on campus. I did not think he was funny, but I had a lot of respect for his game. The boy could ball. As we loaded the bus Tre came up to me and said, "Lav, you straight?" "Yeah, bra," I said, "I'm good." "Do not let them get to you," he said. "They just trying to figure you out. They do not understand that you are not a joker." I chuckled and said, "Tre, it should not be that hard." He laughed and nodded in agreement. I hated the feeling I got when I stepped on the bus because everyone except Johnny and Tre looked at me as if I was not supposed to be there. I started to go sit by the receivers, but then changed my mind. I asked Johnny if I could sit with him because he was the only one I knew who would take care of me in that situation. When the bus took off, I looked out the window put my headphones in and played my gospel music. I immersed myself in my thoughts while gazing over the city of Mobile until we got to the Battle House Hotel. I was so far in my own world that I do not remember who my roommate was. All we had was twenty minutes to put our bags down then we had dinner. As we sat down with others in our positions at these big round tables, it was one big jank-fest with my position. Everyone was going in on everybody; no one was safe at the table. The food was amazing; catfish was the best I had ever tasted in my life. When I bit into the fish, Tim said, "Look at Lav, y'all, biting that fish like a kid from Africa." I did not want to laugh, but I had to admit it was hilarious. When we were finished eating I found out that, we were going to the movies. I was surprised that they were taking us there. This was turning out to be an awesome experience. I planned to have that more consistently, because I would not be on scout team next year. When we got back to the hotel after the movies, we had a night snack and a special teams meeting. That night, after I took my shower and got into the bed, I thought, "This is the start of your career. Do not let everything you have put in to this go to waste. You are not expected to play but just in case, God opens the door for you to get in during a series, you have prepared yourself, so do not tense up. Stay relaxed and make the play. You know the plays; you know your blocking assignments. Just go have fun." That was the last thing I told myself before going to sleep that night. During the pep talk to myself I felt an adrenaline rush because as I was thinking the words I visually saw everything in my head. The next morning when I woke up, I said my morning prayers looked over our game-day test for the special team plays and offensive plays, put my jumpsuit on and went downstairs for breakfast. Again, we all met up at our position table. Coach Stone called our Chaplin to bless the food. After that, we waited for Coach Stone to point and tell us what side of the ball goes to which line before we ate. It was set up like dinner, buffet-style. Following, we had offensive and defensive meetings. Going into the meeting, Coach Rubble immediately took over. We went over the first ten plays they planned to run in the beginning of the game regardless how they line up. Then we went over the second ten plays that were on the script. Coach Rubble called on certain people to make sure everyone understood what was going on at each position. After watching film and going over the plays, we physically walked through the first twenty plays. Following that meeting, we had another meeting for special teams. Then we had a little break, but we had to be back for lunch before we would load the bus at 1 p.m. As we loaded the bus, there was an initial numbness because I did not know what to expect. All year I had been changing in the tent because that is where the scout team players dressed. I could see all the starters locking in and getting ready to play. I could see the coaches' mannerisms as they were getting locked in to call plays and make on-field adjustments. I can remember distinctively looking at Johnny and he had a look of peace and calm. He gave me a smile with a fist pound. I looked at Tre, and his face was calm as well. He had a face of confidence. I looked out of place, because I lacked the focus like everyone else. I did not have that confidence everyone else had. I planned to stay out of the way. I sat by Johnny again, put my headphones in and listened to my gospel music. As we rode to the stadium, I just took everything in. We pulled up to the stadium got off the bus and went straight to the Jag walk. We had to walk around the parking lot while the fans tailgated, shook hands and gave hugs.

It was my first time in the starters' locker room, and I was a little taken aback. They had our jerseys laid out with all new accessories, including new cleats and gloves. I was not used to that because the scout team players got jerseys thrown across a chair and no new accessories. I put my bag down in front of my locker and I went outside to walk on the field. It was my game-day routine. I walked along the sideline, through the end zone, along the other sideline, and then down the middle of the field, just to gather my thoughts about the plays and to mentally run through the plays. After walking the field, I went to get half-dressed before being taped. Then I went back to the field to catch the ball and run the top end of routes. Then I came back in to get fully dressed. The starters were getting hyped for the game. I just took it all in, visually taking in everyone's unique way of getting ready to play. Some were focused on their music, others continued to joke, some rapped with the music playing over the speakers and others just looked chill. I got in my chair closed my eyes with the controlled chaos going on around me and prayed, "God, thank you for this opportunity to play this game. Lord, I pray that no one has an injury; that each team plays tough. Lord, let the best team win. God, allow me to play to the best of my ability. I want to glorify Your name with each play. Lord God, I pray that fans see you and not me when I take the field. God, I am playing like no one is watching but You. I pray this in Your Holy Name. Amen." I opened my eyes just when we were being called to gather for Coach Stone to speak. We said the Lord's Prayer, broke it down and took the field. My teammates started to get rowdy, jumping up and yelling. I was never that type of player. I stayed calm, and as I always had, I moved toward the back of the line.

During the game, I was forced to stay mentally in the game because I was not sure if I was going to play. When the fourth quarter came around Coach Geno came over to me and said, "Lav, go next series." I nodded to him. "All right, Lav, come on, bra. Let's go," Tre said to me. I got in the game and my eyes were wide open like a deer in the headlights.

The game speed was so much faster than it was in practice. And, I thought we moved fast in practice... I thanked God they called plays I knew confidently. The first two plays were power left and power right. The next play was rip strong 560 Houston-hero. I was in the H receiver spot, so I went to everywhere the X receiver went, away from the call. I was on the left side with the X, and I had the hero route. That route was an option route based on the linebacker. The three options were, hitch, in, or out route. All yardages had to be at five yards. As I lined up, I was trying to decide whether I was going to do a hitch or an out. The in-route was not going to happen, because I was not consistent enough to beat them across their face. The quarterback started the cadence, and I looked at the outside linebacker and the corner. It appeared they were in some form of man. He hiked the ball, I exploded off the ball got to the break point and the defender was in the spot. I broke to the out and the quarterback fired the ball to me. I reached out to catch the ball and the linebacker hit me as soon as the ball touched my fingers. Concentrating on securing the catch, I was able to hold on to the ball and stretch out for the first down. Coaches called twelve personnel, so I got up and jogged off the field. When I got to the sideline Vernel said, "Good catch, Lav." Tre said, "Lav, boy, you looked like you was scared." "Man, y'all. I was trying to hold on to the ball. I almost dropped it." We all laughed at my response. Coach Geno came up to me and said with a giggle, "Lav, you got your first college catch. You are big time now." "Thanks, Coach," I said. "Tell the media I am taking questions at the end of the game." He laughed. I was being sarcastic. The game ended, and I knew that would be the last game where I felt out of place.

We finished the season 7-0, and that was the first time I had been a member of an undefeated team. It was a great feeling even if the only time I felt I contributed was during practice and when I was cheering on my teammates on Saturdays. The following Monday, we had our last meeting with our position coach. There had been a rumor going around that Coach Geno was going to leave to join the Auburn staff. As we were about to end the meeting, Coach Geno heard Tim talking about him leaving. "Aye," Coach Geno said, "I don't know what is being said around campus, but I want to tell y'all myself. I am not leaving." When we left that meeting, we knew he was leaving, but it did not bother me, because I was already hip to coaching changes. Tre, Vernel and I spoke about it after we had scheduled our exit meetings with Coach Stone. They said they did not want Coach Geno to leave but understood the circumstances. It would be more money for him, and he would be under the coach he played for back in college. It was common sense that he was leaving. I honestly was somewhat excited about him leaving and with him gone, I might have a real shot at playing. "Either way, God, whatever You want, I am going to roll with Your decision," I thought. God knew I wanted him to go because of his favoritism. Yep, I know that is somewhat harsh, but I am just being honest. When we got the news that Geno had left and gone to Auburn, Vernel and Tre were a little down. I was more worried about my exit meeting coming up with Coach Stone. I did not know what to expect.

When I walked in to my exit meeting, Coach Stone said, "Hey, Bryant, come in. How are you?" "Everything is good Coach," I said. "How is your Mom?" he asked. "She is good, Coach," I said, "Just doing what a mother does." We both giggled. "Good, how are your classes going to finish up?" he asked. "They are going to finish great," I said. "Way better than how I started." "That is always a good thing," he replied. Before the meeting really got started, I sat there and glanced around his huge office. I saw countless awards, game balls and a huge picture of him stretched out making a diving catch. By the time I refocused on him, he was looking down at some paper work. I assumed it was notes about me and what I needed to improve on in the next year. I just sat patiently waiting for him to give me my critique for the year. "Well, Bryant," he said, "You have made great improvement this year. I thought through the summer that you got bigger and stronger. You really developed yourself as a player, because when you came in we felt as a staff that you were a little behind all of the other receivers. The way you worked in the summer and fall, you really pushed to close the gap between you and them. Continue to work and get better. We decided as a staff that we will renew your scholarship, and I think if you continue to improve as you have, you will be fine. Do you have any questions for me?" "No sir," I replied and that was the end of the meeting.

I walked out of the meeting thinking, "That is what Coach Coe and Coach Dean were talking about for the renewal of the scholarship." I walked out of the field house with a push in my spirit to be better the next year. I had already started planning what I was going to do different. I never wanted to feel the pressure of not knowing what would go down in that type of meeting again. A few hours later, we had an emergency meeting at the field house. The Athletic Director, Dr. Costa, called the meeting. He was a very clean-cut, straightforward man with high expectations. As we walked into the team room, Dr. Costa shook the hand of everyone on the team. When everyone got into the meeting room, he started talking, "Good evening, gentlemen. I wanted to congratulate you all on a perfect season. People can say what they want about the teams you played, but they cannot take away that you were undefeated, not to mention this was our first year with a football program. Not many schools can say that when they first started a football program, they went undefeated. I believe that deserves a reward, so everyone is getting a ring as a reward for that dedication and hard work. Now, let's see if we can continue this trend for years to come." Next, the Balfour ring rep walked in. Internally, I was going crazy because I had never experienced anything like that event. Some of my teammates had multiple state championship rings and knew what it felt like. To have the opportunity to experience that was amazing. Everyone was fitted for the rings. It was a fantastic way to end the day.

The only thing left now was to finish my final exams and go home for Christmas break. My last final exam was the next day. I knew I would do great on it, because I had studied. I was ready to go home, because it had been six months. When I got home, I talked to my Mom for an hour. She asked about my grades, how Vernel and Tre were doing, and the typical questions parents ask when you come home for break during your first year of college. After that, I went straight to Gulfport High to see Coach Coe. I walked into his office and he said, "Well, well, well. Hey, everybody, look it is Bryant Lavender." I laughed and gave him a hug. "How did you finish with your grades?" he said. "I finished great," I said. "I will have a 3.0 GPA when grades are posted." "OK," he said, "how did football finish?" "It finished great as well," I said. "We went undefeated, and we are getting rings." "Really?" he said. "Rings? I will tell you, Bryant, that is very rare what you all have done. That is first-class of Stone and Costa deciding to get you all rings. That says a lot about how they are directing the program. Now, tell me how you finished on the season." "I finished pretty well," I said. "I got better and had a chance to travel to the second-to-last game. I had one catch for five yards." He looked at me with a sterner face and said, "Bryant, how are you really doing over there? Are you working hard in the weight room and the practice field?" "Yes, sir, I am," I said. "Other than hating to be on scout team, I am putting forth every effort to be the player I know I can be. Do you know something that I do not?" "Well," he said, "I called Chavo one day and asked how you were doing over there." He started to chuckle a little bit, shook his head and said, "I cannot stand that guy; he always walked around like his stuff doesn't stink." "Coach," I interjected, "what did he say?" "He told me that you are not the athlete they thought they signed," he said. My heart sank. Coach Coe continued, "That they do not think you will be a playmaker or a starter for the program. That you would be there just to make sure that the team GPA does not fall." I kept my composure and said, "Oh, really, that is what he said, huh?" I giggled a little bit. "Bryant," Coach Coe said, "do you know what is a slap in my face? That is telling me I cannot and do not know talent. That is saying I was never a good coach. How dare he disrespect me like that. Bryant, promise me that you will work your tail off on and off the field. When you become a starter and then a playmaker, you smile in those coaches' faces but do not trust them. When you leave and become successful, you can say they did not believe in you." I looked him in his eyes and said, "I promise, Coach." "Bryant," he said, "make them respect you through your hard work and consistency in making plays. Remind yourself they do not think you are the player they thought you were and every day make them eat those words." "Yes, sir," I replied. That conversation put everything into overload. As I left his office, all I could do was think about every word he had just told me. It brought everything done to me in the spring back into perspective. I understood the reason I was treated so badly. The reason I was treated like a scrub was because that was what they thought I was. It all made sense. Every day I was home for Christmas, I ran routes and caught the football.

I also played flag with my friends. My focus was to come back better than ever before. It was church and football, the only two things on my mind. In that order, I was still hearing God's voice when He told me to go to work.

While I was home, I saw Coach Lute at the local all-star game hosted at our high school football stadium and he said, "Bryant, how are you, big'n'?" "I am well, Coach. How are you?" I replied. "Blessed," he said, "thanks for asking; hey, look, I want you to give me a call. I would like to talk to you about some possibilities." He handed me his card. "All right, Coach I will," I responded as he gave me his card. I thought it was a bit strange, but I would be a man of my word and give him a call, so on Monday I decided to give him a call around noon, "Coach Lute, It is Bryant. How are you?" "B-Lav," he said, "Everything is good on my end. What about you?" "All is well, Coach," I said. "Is it really?" he asked. "Are they treating you OK over at South Alabama?" "Yes," I said, "everything is fine, nothing to complain about." I was wondering what he was trying to get at. "Bryant," he said, "I called over there and asked about you. They do not believe in you. They told me that you will not play. Why not transfer here where we can take care of you? We know you are a playmaker. If you come down here you would only have to spend one year to graduate and you will be able to go to any school in the country because that is how good I know you are. What do you say to that?" "I do not know, Coach," I said. "I know everything has not been what I expected at South, but I am not sure I should leave." "What do you mean?" he said. "I can guarantee you will play here. That you will go to a major university after one year. They told me that you will not play at South, but you are better than them. Come be a Lion where you know you will get treated fairly." What he said was sweet music to my ears, "OK, Coach," I said. "Let me think about it." "Call me back in two days," he said. I got off the phone realizing I really disliked my first semester at South. Maybe Coach Lute was right. I can transfer and go to another school. I did not deserve to be treated like that. I started to think about all the possibilities of what would happen after I transferred.

Pastor Gee had preached a message that came back into my mind. "Don't run from this situation," was the statement that stuck out most in my mind. "You think going somewhere else will be better, but it will not. Do not un-plant yourself; you will only delay what God is doing in you." I thought about what Coach Coe had said to me days before. I still did not know what to do. That night, I prayed to God, "Lord, tell me what to do. Me, personally, I kind of want to transfer, and I kind of want to stay. I am torn on what I should do. Nevertheless, I am coming to You because You know what is best for me. You were the one who told me to go to South. Tell me what to do." I sat in silence for a few minutes waiting for Him to speak. He said, "Stay." That made my decision. The next day I called Coach Lute and told him I was going to stay at South. He was a little displeased with my decision and said, "When they do you wrong just give me a call and

I won't tell you I told you so." I looked up at the ceiling and said, "OK, God. Let's make it happen at South. Whatever you need me to be, I will be."

Shortly after, I received a text from Vernel about who our new receiver coach would be. Coach Joe Simp, who had played at Colorado State. He was leaving from University of Arkansas to come coach us. Immediately I thanked God for giving me a fresh start with a new position coach. If I had transferred, I would not have that opportunity. That gave me a boost in my faith that God takes care of everything for His children. We would meet Coach Simp at the beginning of spring practice. In the meantime, Coach Stone would take over the receivers. When we returned back to school, the only thing we had was weights for football. In the meantime, I would wake up early every morning to pray and encourage myself. I would go into the bathroom and say to myself, "You will not tolerate disrespect. You are the best receiver here. People will respect you. When you walk in the room, the atmosphere will change. You are the head and not the tail, above and not beneath. You are more than a conqueror. You are a victor." I spoke those words to myself every day, and I began to see change in myself. My walk changed. My talk changed, and people began to respect me. Right after one of the first lifting sessions we had, Tim called all the receivers up for a meeting in the locker room. "Aye," he said, "y'all, I just wanted to get us together real quick. We have to be great this season. No excuses, we need everyone to be on top of their game. Coach Geno is gone, so we have to take care of one another. I will be the enforcer if I have to. Y'all know I am not afraid to fight, and I will fight everyone of y'all just to get you to do right. Make sure y'all are going to class; we cannot get ineligible 'cause of class. I will be checking your classes and if you are not in there, you will have to see me. Real talk." "You make sure you are in class," I blurted out. Tim said, "What, Lav?" "You make sure you going to class, too," I said. "Do not miss your class to make sure we are in class. You be accountable as well." Tim nodded, shook my hand and said, "That's real, Lav." We broke it down and the meeting was over. As we were walking out of the front door, Tre asked, "Lav, what were you going to do if Tim would have snapped on you and tried to fight?" "I would have fought him. Probably would have lost, but I was going to throw hands with him." We both fell out laughing and got into the car.

A few weeks later I saw Coach Simp in the field house. I walked by his office door to see if it was open, and it was. I knocked on the door. "Yes?" a real calm voice said. "Hey, Coach Simp, I am Bryant Lavender." "Ah, yes," he said, "from Gulfport, Mississippi. Will be a redshirt freshman this year. Also known as 'Lav' correct?" I was shocked he knew all of that already, "Yes, sir," I said, "I know you are busy moving in and getting settled, I just wanted to introduce myself." He got up from his desk, extended his hand for me to shake it, "Joe Simp," he said, "nice to meet you. I will be calling a meeting tomorrow. Are you ready to work?" "Yes, sir," I said confidently, "I always am." He smiled and said, "OK, I like to hear that. We will see shortly." I laughed as I walked out of the office.

The next day we had a 4 p.m. meeting scheduled to meet with our position coach. When we got in our meeting room I assumed he would be in there already, but he was not. He walked in a few minutes after everyone else and the chatter ceased when he walked in. Everyone put eyes on him. He was about 5-feet, 9-inches tall, light-skin and baldheaded with freckles. "Good afternoon, men. My name is Joe Simp," he said. "I will be your receiver coach. I am originally from Beaumont, Texas. Played my college ball at Colorado State graduated with a B.S. in exercise science and I have a master's in the same thing. I started my coaching career there as well. From there I went to Elon University, then Wofford, and before I got here, I was at the University of Arkansas. I am excited to be here with you all. The way I coach is very detailed; I will show you every possible form of coverage you will ever see at this level. I expect everyone to work as hard as the next man, and you must know your assignments and execute them. I like to run a rotation system. For me the first string and second string are classified as starters, because you will get about the same amount of reps in the game. The most important thing for a receiver is to be able to run fast over, over and over again. The way we do that is keep everybody fresh. Finally, if you do not block, you will not play for me. It is as simple as that." When Coach Simp finished the last sentence, I knew I would play now. "Thank you, God," I thought. I would have a legit shot now. "Guys, I do this everywhere I go. I want you all to think of five words that make a good teammate. We will write them on the board. Then, because you said these words, I expect everyone will live up to them." The first word that came to my mind was trustworthy. "All right, give me what you got." Everyone started blurting out words, and we had some people who had synonyms for words. The five words we ended up with were accountable, dependable, confident, hard-worker and trustworthy. "All right, men," he said. "Now that we have the intro stuff out of the way, it is time to go to work." With that, Coach Simp had calmly concluded the meeting.

Next week was the first day of spring practice. We always had a meeting before we got on the field. Coach Simp wanted to make sure everyone was on time and accounted for. He made it clear for the first day that he wanted us to fly around and have fun. If we needed a breather, the rule was to tap the top of our helmet to get someone else in. Tim asked, "Coach, who is the first group, second group? Like, how are we supposed to know when we go?" "For today," Coach Simp said, "go in the groups that you have been going in, but they will change tomorrow. Fellas, when I first got here everyone tried to tell me who needed to start, wanted me to watch film, but I did not listen or watch. I want to see for myself who will be my top wideouts. Everyone hear me very clearly, no one has the upper hand. The spots are all open, so if you want to be in the top eight receivers, show me, starting today." I turned up in my spirit, because I was about to be in that top eight.

cause I had put in the work. The next day, just as Coach said, the depth chart was up and I had moved up four spots. During the second week of spring, we lost some receivers due to them being ineligible or them just quitting. The X-receiver position was cut down to just two deep because of that. I was now third on the depth chart for H-receiver, but I wanted to go X because that is what I played in high school and I knew I was better than second man at the X-spot. One day, I talked to Tre about moving to outside receiver after practice. He felt that it would be a good move for me. I thought so, too. I did not have anything to lose. I had already been brushing up on the outside receiver routes. I was very confident that I could make a smooth transition back out there on the island. The next day, right before we went to the field, I stopped by Coach Simp's office and said, "Hey, Coach, I was wondering if I could move to X?" "Why?" he asked. I was not expecting that question back, and said, "Because, I played there in high school. I am more comfortable out there. I also will have a better chance to get on the field." Coach Simp did not answer back right away but after a few seconds passed said, "I will ask Coach Rubble and see if he is OK with it. Take reps at both today and if you need help at the X-spot, I will be right there." "Yes, sir!" I said enthusiastically. "That might be a good move for you," Coach Simp said as I walked out of his office. When I walked into the locker room to finish getting dressed Tre and Vernel were waiting. "Lav, what did he say?" Tre asked me. "To work both X-spot and H-spot today. He would ask Coach Rubble about the move, and it might be a good move for me." "Oh, shoot, Lav, you in there," Tre said. "You better kill, so you can stay out there." I was excited to be back outside on the island.

We had a scrimmage that Saturday that really solidified the X-spot for me. I went with the third string, because Coach Simp wanted to give my teammate one more shot to keep the second-string spot. During my series on the field, I ran a thirteen-yard curl and turned it into a sixty-yard touchdown. Once again, everyone was shocked, but I was not and neither was Coach Simp. Shortly after I got back over to our sideline, Tre told me Coach Geno was at the scrimmage. He walked up to me and said, "Lav, what up man?" "What up, Coach?" I replied. "They said you just scored a touchdown," he said. "Yep, I did," I said. "Finally gave me a fair chance to show what I can do." Tre was listening to what I said and giggled a little bit. "Well, I knew you always had it in you," he said. "I was trying to pull it out." "Oh, OK, right," I said sternly and walked away. When the scrimmage was over, Tre came to me and said, "Lav, why did you act like that with Geno?" "'Cause, man," I said, "he always trying to play me like I suck. I do not fool with him on the football tip." "I know, man," Tre said, "but you do not have to talk to him like that. That was a little disrespectful." I know it was, but I just felt some type of way about how he had treated me. He also did not know that I had been working to change my mindset. Everything was about to change for me and I knew it.

The meeting we had on Monday before practice was different, Coach Simp walked in and played what, in his opinion, were the top four plays from the scrimmage, and I noticed that he chose three of my plays. Coach Simp posed the question, "Why do you all think Lav works so hard?" I got nervous because he put me on blast. My teammates looked back at me and started laughing. He asked again, "Why do you all think Lav works so hard?" Again, they laughed. I waited for a few seconds then answered, "Because I do not have a spot." My teammates busted out laughing, but Coach Simp cut them off and said, "Do not laugh. He is right, but I tell you this, he will play for me. Lav, keep working." I nodded to his statement. That encouraged me so much. It was confirmation from God that I was on the right path. I finished the spring and was awarded as the most improved player. I was surprised. I was not expecting to receive that award, but I was happy to be recognized. Coach Stone addressed the team and said, "Men, this was a great spring for us. I believe we made great strides to be prepared for the fall. We have our evaluations on everyone. Let us continue to get better every day and take ahold of the great push for the summer. Men let's finish strong in the classroom this semester. Make sure you take care of business." Receivers had a small meeting after we broke it down as a team. "Men, this was a great spring, but we still have a lot of work to do." We broke it down and headed to the locker room. "Lav, come here," Coach Simp called me over. "What's up, Coach?" I asked curiously. "Great job this spring," he said. "Way to work. Make sure you keep it up, and congrats on getting that award."

I did finish strong in my academics, and I took care of scheduling for fall and spring. When I met with my academic advisor for physical therapy, my major, she told me that I would have to miss some games once I got accepted into the program for my junior and senior year. There would be clinical sessions that I would not be able to miss. When I heard that, I spoke up, "Excuse me, I do not mean to interrupt you, but I know right now that I have to change my major. Football pays for everything, and missing games will not fly for that." She politely gave me the papers I needed to declare a major change, and I stood up and marched out of her office. I went straight to my athletic advisor to inform her what had happened and declared my new major as exercise science. We set up every class I would take all the way through graduation. We even wrote in what teachers I needed to take.

When we came back for the summer, I made a plan to do extra work on the field. Tre, Vernel and I also moved into the Grove Apartments. We became official roommates; in the Grove, the room was fully furnished. First day back we all sat in the living room and had a pow-wow to explain what we wanted to accomplish that season. I expressed to the fellas I could not sit on the bench that year. That I would be putting massive amounts of extra fieldwork in, and I would love them to join me. They agreed to put in work with me and gave me an extra push. God could not have given me any two better friends to room with. I knew that year would be great for us all.

The 2010 summer was awesome for me. I began to become the player I wanted to be. I was getting bigger, faster and stronger. The extra work was helping, too, and Tre and Vernel were right along with me. I enjoyed every bit of the summer, and I knew it was because I had truly embraced what God was doing and allowed Him to work his plan for that chapter in my life. We put countless hours in on the field outside of what we were scheduled to do. The last two weeks we took a break from extra work. We also had a new GA come in to help with receivers. His name was Hallywood. He looked very familiar. It was not until we found out that he had gone to Hoover and had been on the TV show called, "Two a Days," that it clicked. He had been their major receiver and he was a beast. He never dropped the ball, and always made the play for his team when they needed him to. I faithfully watched that show, so it was cool to meet him. Hallywood and I formed a great relationship in the short time he had been at South. I picked his brain as much as possible asking any and everything about football. I also asked him how it was being on TV. He was a man of few words unless Coach Simp put him in charge of coaching for a day. He was cutting my hair one day when I asked him, "Aye, Coach," I said, "can I ask you something?" "Yeah, man," he said, "what's up?" "I do not know how long you will be here," I said, "but for your duration here will you push me, show me everything you know?" He giggled at first and said, "Lav, bra, you good. Just keep working." "I know," I said, "but I need you to pull everything out of me." "All right, Lav, I got you," he said. "Appreciate that," I replied. I knew he would not be with us long because of the connections he had, and I wanted to grasp all I could from him.

Questions

1. When times get tough, have you allowed God to speak?
2. Do you trust the process that God is taking you through?

CHAPTER 7

Prove God Right:
Be Who God Told You To Be, Not Who They Say You Are

REDSHIRT FRESHMAN YEAR

Fall camp could not have started any worse for someone who had put in the amount of work I had put in over the summer. The first day with pads, I dropped everything. I only remember catching five balls. "Lav, bra, catch the dang ball. What's wrong with you? We put in too much work for you to be looking that bad," Tre was getting on me. "Bra," I said, "I do not know what is wrong." He did not have to get on to me. I was getting on myself. It had gotten to the point that I told the quarterback to stop throwing me the ball. Vernel overheard me say that to the quarterback and said, "Lav, what's wrong, bra? Why did you tell the quarterback not to throw you the ball?" I looked at him, shook my head and said, "Bra, you see the balls I have dropped?" "Tre," he said, "did you hear this dude? He told the quarterback not to throw the ball to him anymore. Talk to your boy, man." They just started laughing, "My boy, Lav, down bad today," Tre said. I could not do anything but shake my head and laugh. I was ready to get that practice over with, because it was just that bad for me. Coach Simp called us up after practice and said, "How was practice for us as whole?" No one answered. "Not bad as a whole," he said. "Just remember, fellas, we have to spark the offense. How did you all do individually?" "Horrible," I blurted out. A few laughs followed my statement, "That is why we have film," Coach Simp said. "It is never as bad as it seems, and it is never as good as it seems." Before we broke it down, Coach Hallywood made it over to the group where he yelled, "Lav, we are catching balls after this. Do not go to the locker room." I nodded, because I needed to get out of that funk and fast. I ran over to the ball bag after we broke it down and Coach Hallywood said, "All right, Lav, I need a hundred catches straight. You drop one, you have to start over." As we went through the ball drills, I caught all of the balls. "Lav, why didn't you do this in practice?" Coach Hallywood asked. "Coach," I said, "I do not know. What was I doing wrong?" "Watching the ball to the tuck," he said. "You did not watch the ball during the tuck like you are doing now." "OK, Coach," I answered. "Tomorrow, Lav, we need a better day," he said.

There were no more bad days during camp after that practice. I caught everything after I fixed what he said I needed to fix. I was watching the ball all the way in to the tuck. Every day I caught extra balls after practice to reinforce that technique. Before I knew it, I was being interviewed for an article in the newspaper. The headline read, "Lavender catching on for the Jaguars." The article appeared after the first scrimmage we had during fall camp. Here is what the coaches had to say about me, "I thought Bryant Lavender had a great day at receiver. He broke tackles and made some big plays. He has really earned it. He's worked his tail off this summer, and you can tell by the look in his eyes he really wants to make something happen," Coach Stone said. When Coach Rubble was asked about the offense, he mentioned my name, "Our best offensive player in the preseason has been Lavender. Heck, he has been our best football player. He's improved greatly and is putting pressure on Tim Jackson." When Coach Simp was asked about me, he said, "He's had a great camp. He is a guy going back to the spring to make the most out of every rep. He's someone out of the group who has made the most out of his opportunities. Starting in the spring when I got here no one talked about Bryant Lavender. I really did not have a good idea who he was and what he could do. But every rep, he was full-speed. And when a kid like that is going full speed every rep you notice him." The reporter wrote in the article, "That is high praise for a player only playing four of the seven games last year with one reception for five yards." How refreshing it was for my hard work to manifest before my eyes. As long as I did my part, God did the rest.

The first game of the 2010 season was against Pikeville College. That time I was traveling to the hotel. That time I knew I was playing. That time I allowed my family and friends to come. That is truly when my career started in my eyes. Coach Simp pulled me to the side after walk-through and said, "Lav, you have earned everything you have. You have worked hard and will get your shot Saturday to make plays. Continue to make the best of your opportunities." "Yes, sir," I answered with a smile. I was able to hold my composure on the outside, but on the inside, I was so amped for Saturday. Vernel, Tre and I were all traveling this year. That added to the adrenaline rush I had. As I got into my regular routine at the stadium all I could think was, "Dad, I am here. I am about to be on TV like I told you way back when." A few tears rolled down my face as that thought replayed in my mind. The nerves were stronger than ever. Not only was that the day I would fulfill one promise I had made to my Dad years ago, but also my family, Coach Coe and friends were in the stands that day. Before we took the field, I prayed, "Father God, thank you for the strength to get to this point. Lord, let the fans see You and not me. I play for You and only You. God, allow me to remember every play and execute them to the best of my ability. In Jesus' name, I pray. Amen."

We took the field and the butterflies were raging until I participated in the first play. On the first drive, Coach Simp said, "Stay close, someone needs a breather." We opened up with one running play followed by three passing plays. On the passing plays, Tim had all go-routes. "Lav, go," Coach Simp said. Coach signaled the play Lucky 60 mills

X-follow. For that play call, the X was the first read. As I lined up, Johnny called my name, "Bryant, I have the whip route to clear it out for you right?" I nodded my head yes although I could not believe he said the play out loud like that. I looked at the structure of the defense and saw they were in man coverage. At the snap of the ball, the corner played mirror technique. I stemmed inside, and he tried to wash me down but I held my position. I got to my breaking point and stuck my foot in the ground to run my dig. I gave him a flipper with my elbow, and I looked toward the quarterback. I saw the release of the ball in my direction; the ball was coming to me. I caught the ball and immediately turned up field. I broke the tackle of the corner that was holding me, and exploded toward the end zone, raced down the field and got horse-collared at the one-yard line. I jumped up and pointed in the section of the stands where my family and friends were sitting, and they went crazy. Teammates came to celebrate with me and congratulate me on the play. "Lav," one of them said, "you were supposed to score that, bra. You cannot get caught at the one." "I know, man," I replied to my teammate. "Why didn't you dive?" he asked. "Bra, I do not know," I said, "I was just … man, I don't know." I was trying to catch my breath. "Black boy, way to make a play," Tre said coming up behind me. "Lav, good play, bra," Vernel said coming up after him. After that play, the game flew by as we beat Pikeville. I finished the game with personal high four catches for sixty-seven yards. God allowed me to perform to the best of my ability. After the game I went straight to Coach Coe and said, "Hey, Coach, thanks for coming." He had a stern look on his face and said, "What do you call that thing you did after you made that catch? You need to act like you have been there before." "I know. I know, Coach. I was a little bit excited," I answered. He smiled and said, "You played a great game. I am proud of you." "Thanks, Coach," I said with a big smile on my face. Next, I went to see my family, "Bryant, are you riding home with us?" my Mom asked. "Yes, Ma'am," I said. "Otherwise, I will not get to my room until late." Bernard and John were there and I went to speak with them before we had to go into the locker room. That day was just great all the way round. Vernel, Tre and I got to play in the game. Our families, friends and coaches came to watch us play, and we got the win.

Sunday during film, Coach Simp asked a question that changed the way I looked at football for the rest of my life. He always made us evaluate ourselves. When my play from the game came up, he said, "Lav, what is wrong with your route?" He replayed it so I could look at the play again. When I watched the play over again nothing came to mind. "Um, I could have done better with my release," I said unsurely. "No, your release was fine. Look again," he said replaying the play. I did not see what he was talking about, "I don't know, Coach." "All right let's dissect it," he said, "how many yards is the dig route?" "Twelve yards," I replied. "Correct, let's see if you went twelve yards." He put the play on slow motion, and we all counted the yards. He stopped the film when I began to break toward the dig. "Eleven and a half yards, Lav. You are half a yard short," Coach Simp said. I scrunched my face up at first but then I understood what he was saying. "Fellas, depth is important. That half a yard could have been the difference between a first down and a turnover, win or a loss. My point is for you to pay attention to detail." It was as if God was saying through him, "Pay attention to my rules. Abide by rules in the full capacity." If I had followed the rules and gone twelve yards like we practiced, that might have been my first career touchdown for the University of South Alabama. "One other thing, Lav, next time you make a big play, celebrate with your teammates. Whoever you are pointing to in the stands does not matter. They did not help you make the play. They were not there when you practiced, but your teammates were so celebrate with the people who were there during the fire." "Yeah, Coach. That is my bad. That will not happen again," I answered.

Instead, my first career touchdown came against Edward Waters. We were in the red zone, Coach Rubble called double slants, and the quarterback threw it to me. That team was not good at all, we blew them out. I only played two quarters. I wanted to score against a team that was more challenging for us. I had a chance to do that against Georgia State, who was also a first-year program as we had been the year before. During the third quarter, I was able to be the spark that Coach Simp mentioned during camp. Tim and I started rotating offensive series, and it was my turn to go. When Coach Rubble called the play, he tagged it with X-post. In Coach Rubble's offense, anytime your position received a tag on play the rule was you had to win. The one thing I loved about the system that we ran is the options and variations on the routes. Based on the defensive back alignment after the ball was snapped we had the freedom to go under or over the defender. It was very simple but effective for us. As I lined up and looked at my triangle I could see that the defensive back was about eight yards off, flat footed and facing me. At the snap of the ball, he did not backpedal. He stayed flat-footed with a slight inside technique. "He is beat," I thought. I went over the top of him, the quarterback threw the ball, and I caught it for a touchdown. That time I did not look in the stands. I celebrated with my teammates. I finished the game with four catches and a touchdown. "Lav, bra, you balled out today, boy. Where did that come from?" Tre asked. "All that work we put in during the summer," I replied and he smiled as we dapped one another up. Coach Hallywood came up behind me, hit my shoulder pads and said, "Great work today, Lav. Keep it up." Media relations informed me when I went back to the locker room that they needed me for a postgame interview. When I entered into the media room, there were cameras and lights everywhere. As I took my seat at the table I thought, "So this is what it feels like to do this. I am good on this if only just to get out of those pads." My thoughts were soon interrupted by a reporter, who said, "Lavender, you had a big game for the Jags. What do you think set you up for the big game you had?" "Well, my teammates," I said, "especially the offensive line. They held up long enough for the quarterback to get the ball to me."

"This year has been a great one for you in general, what did you do different from a year ago?" The reporter asked. "I just fully adjusted to the system," I said. "I bought into what we are doing here at South Alabama. Put in the work, and it is just coming out now."

The next week was really big for us, because we were playing U.C. Davis in California. That was the first game we were traveling far to. They also had a history of being a winning program. That was a big game for me because it would be the first time my family on the west coast would be able to see me play. During the game we were in a position we had never been in before. Coach Simp kept me out of the game during my series, but I had played in the game so it did not bother me that much. I had been contributing the whole season. Why could I not be in the game when it mattered? I put my pride aside because at the end of the day I wanted us to win the game. It was not until midway through the fourth quarter when the momentum shifted into our favor after the defense created a turnover. It took us the rest of the fourth quarter to drive down into the red zone. Tim caught the game-winning touchdown on a red zone fade route. We rushed the field as if we had won the national championship.

During the meeting on Sunday, after I got my evaluation from the game, I realized why I did not play much. It really blew my mind when I saw how many offensive snaps I had. Seven, I only had seven offensive snaps. I was so upset, because I had put in to be trusted in those types of situations. After the meeting, Coach Simp said, "Lav, stay for a second." I waited for everyone to leave the room before seeing what he wanted to talk about. "Lav," he said, "don't let what happened in the game get to you. I know you did not play as much as you should have. It had nothing to do with your play because you have been playing well. Coach Rubble and Coach Stone wanted Tim to stay in the game." I nodded and said, "OK, Coach." It still bothered me, but it made me respect him even more for explaining what had happened. That actually gave me a push to finish the season strong mentally. We again went undefeated. Seventeen wins and zero losses. I had never been a part of a team with a two-year win streak. There was a certain confidence you have with being undefeated. I, for the first time in my life, could say in my first two years of college, I went without a loss and had the hardware to prove it.

Coach Simp gave us a questionnaire sheet to fill out on how we saw ourselves. There were two questions, "What level did you perform on this year? What level do you plan to perform on by the time you leave South?" Coach Simp challenged us to give an honest assessment on the type of player we were at that point and the type of player we wanted to become. The answers I circled were starter and All-American. During the exit meeting I had with him he pulled the sheet out for reference. "Lav, I saw you circled starter and All-American. What do you have to do to reach your goal?" he asked. "Continue to do what I have been doing. Being a great teammate and making plays," I answered. "Lav, based on what I have seen and what I have heard, you are on the right track. As long as you continue to do what you are doing and whatever else is needed along with favor from God, you will reach your goal." "Thanks, Coach," I said with a smile. "You have caught a slant. Go, dig, and come back," he said. "You need to catch a post, shallow, curl and a double move route." I nodded to what he said. "Lav, that is all I have for you. Keep up the good work." I left the meeting feeling encouraged. The exit meeting with Coach Stone was even shorter than that. He let me know that I was getting my scholarship renewed and that I had had a good season.

REDSHIRT SOPHOMORE YEAR

When I came back for the spring after the fall, I felt stronger than ever. I was number one on the depth chart since Tim was graduating in May. Over the Christmas break Coach Coe told me to keep working because the journey was not over, that what they said about me is still in their minds. Every day, I replayed it in my mind, which compelled me to go that much harder. One day after workouts I had a letter from Coach Stone that read, "Bryant, I'm so proud of you the way you have matured as a player and person over the last two years. I know you have had some roadblocks in your life, but you have chosen not to let that keep you from achieving your goals. I admire that." That added fuel to my desire to be what others said I could not be. When I got back to my room, I put Coach Stone's letter in my memorabilia box. The spring was great for me. I secured my spot and built my confidence to an all-time high as a player.

I knocked on Coach Benny's office door and he waved me in, "Coach, I apologize for blowing up on you this morning. I was taking up for my team, but there was a better way to do it. I should not have disrespected you like that." There was about ten second pause before he answered, "Lav, you know I love you, brother. I accept your apology. The only reason I snapped back at you like that was because you put me in that position. I was walking around telling the team that they could change their grip; I just had not gotten to your team." I nodded my head in agreement, to what he was saying. "Brother," Coach Benny said, "you know I do not play favorites. I have so much respect for you because I know you have busted your butt to get here. We are family, and family fights with one another, but we reconcile grow from it and get stronger." "Yes sir," I said, "thank you for accepting my apology." "Always man," Coach responded getting out of his seat to give me a hug. After we had our conversation I knew that we would never have a misunderstanding again.

After the big argument with Coach Benny blew over, it was time to get ready for the fall. Going into the beginning of the fall, I was slated as the starter. On the depth chart, my name was on the first line, and no one treated me like a scrub anymore. I got first dibs on the new helmets, gloves and cleats that we were ordering. I even tested the new

Nike gloves when the rep came by our school. I did not change my helmet, though. I wanted to keep my revolution for two reasons. One, it reminded me that I earned everything I was getting now, and two, I have always thought they were the coolest helmets on the planet. I changed the version of my cleats and gloves because I could now get the ones I wanted.

During camp, a reporter interviewed me about being the number one guy, but none of that mattered because I still had to work for my spot. In the back of my mind, I knew it could be taken away just as fast as it was given to me. I was the second leading receiver last year and the reporter was asking questions about how we would do this year after losing Tim to the NFL. I said that everyone was working hard, that everyone would step up and that we would make plays still. That year we had North Carolina State and Kent State on the schedule. They were the big games because they were strong teams in their conferences.

During the first week of the season I had an interview with media relations. It felt like I was on ESPN's "30 For 30." I thought it was the traditional Q and A they do before the game to put it in the program on game day. When I got to the office, I found out that it was going in the program for game day, but it was the feature story. The interviewer asked questions about how I got started in football, how long I had been playing. He asked about my Dad passing, how that changed my life, and how big of a part that played in who I was at that point. The one question that stuck out to me the most was, "Bryant, what is one of the other reasons why you push yourself the way that you do?" I sat silent for a few seconds to visualize it in order to put it into words. "There are a lot of guys where I am from who were great athletes, but when they went to college they stopped playing. My bigger purpose is to show kids that no matter what anybody says or how many chips are against them, they can keep fighting and know when they are God's child. He will help them find their way; it may not be when they want it, but He's always on time." Friday night when we were at the hotel, I spoke with God while I was lying in bed. "God," I said, "look how You worked everything out for me. Never allow me to get the big head. God, I do not want to get all 'Hollywood.' God, I want to walk with kings and keep my common touch. Isn't that what the poem said? God, allow me to handle the limelight correctly." Tears trickled down my face, because it had been a hard road to get there. I thought all the way back to the promise I had made to my father. God has allowed me to continue to fulfill that promise. Because I am a believer and followed the principles he set before me to be a division one-football player. God gave me a desire of my heart. Wiping my tears away I said, "Thank you, God," and went to sleep.

Game Day 2011 was here. As we got on the bus to head to the stadium, everything was new for me all over again. This year everyone looked at me and I was accepted. I belonged. This year I had the chance to share my seat with a teammate who was traveling for the first time. I got to show the agape love of Jesus Christ. That time, coaches came to me and asked if I was ready to play. That time I was expected to make plays. Before we took the field, I gave a speech, "This right here," I said, "this is for everybody that said we couldn't do nothing, bra. They said we couldn't win, we were sorry, we have two rings but that doesn't mean nothing, bra. This right here, right here, this is the beginning of history. This season right here is the beginning of history. Can't anyone stop us because nobody works harder than us. Let's go!" After I said my piece, I sat down and prayed. There was a chip on my shoulder. I had to prove I belonged. I went out and played as if no one was watching but God. We won the game 20-10 for the season-opener. I finished the game with three catches for fifty-five yards. After that game everything really took off like a rocket when it came to fan popularity. All the kids wanted all my stuff. I made bargains with them for the next week that I would bring a pair of gloves for them. I gave away my towel every game. The enthusiasm on their faces was amazing. Reporters asked me to do more and more interviews. On campus, I tried to hide even more because my regular clothes did not do the trick anymore. I did love sitting with regular students in the cafeteria and talking about life, where they were from, and their majors. My prayer evolved to asking God to show me how to use my influence for His will.

The week of the N.C. State game, the campus was on fire. Everyone had tons of questions, but Coach Simp really kept us focused for the biggest game in program history. At the time, N.C. State had the number one defensive backfield in the country. Their entire defensive backfield was projected to get drafted. I was excited because how many times do you get to play against the top-rated defensive backfield? During the meetings, Coach Simp said, "Do not be intimidated. They are people just like you. You are prepared. Just go play football." Once we got to Raleigh, the butterflies began to come. I looked at Tre and Vernel and said, "Boys, how y'all feeling?" "Bra, I'm big chilling," Vernel replied. "Lav, don't talk to me, I still sleepy," Tre said. Vernel and I laughed and we started talking about the city. We did our walk through and went to the hotel and ate dinner and had meetings. The next day when we got to the stadium before the game I took in the sight of their beautiful stadium. During warm ups it started to rain. Coach Simp called us up and said, "Don't worry about the grass, it will not give way. It is the best grass money can buy." That calmed my nerves that had started to get to me. We finished warm ups and went in the locker room, and I went to talk to God. "Lord," I said, "calm me down please. I don't want to be too anxious. Give me the grace to act as if I have been there before. God, give me the ability to play with your passion. Amen." When we went back out on the field, the stadium was filled with 60,000 people. When they announced our names, we were booed by the N.C. State fans. Vernel hit Tre and me on the shoulder and said, "Aye, boys, this is what we signed the scholarship for! Have fun today, boys." We dapped one another up and ran out of the tunnel. When they announced the home team, the stadium erupted. The wolf howled as we saw the home team walking and swaying out of their tunnel. That was when my adrenaline came back. I thought, "Let's go, Lav. Make plays!" We won the toss and chose to receive the ball. The first play was X-follow, and I had the dig route again. I lined up and looked at my triangle. They were in Cover 3. Before the snap the thought, "Get your depth," popped into my head. The quarterback hiked the ball; I exploded off the ball, got to my depth, and made the catch. First down, Jags. After that play I said to myself, "Oh yeah, it on man. Let's go, Lav, make plays!" The wolf pack was as advertised. They defeated us 35-13 and gave us our first lost in program history.

The following week we were to play Kent State. When I walked into the meeting room early and saw the Jacksonville Jaguars scout watching film, at first I was nervous, but then I started talking to him. He was a very laid back and cool individual. Right before the meeting, the rest of the receivers filed into the room. Coach B came in to get the scout. When he asked about us as a group, Coach B responded while pointing at each of us and telling the scout a little bit about each of us. While pointing at me, he said, "That is Bryant Lavender; he definitely will be able to play at the next level for you all. He follows all the rules and is a leader. He will do anything you ask him, and he makes a bunch of plays for us." I was surprised he had so many great things to say about me. The scout looked at me and nodded his head toward me, and they both left. "Lav, Coach B, put you in the game for real," Tre said aloud and our other teammates were just as shocked as I was. I just thought, "I appreciate that, God."

At the game, everyone was a little uneasy about our first loss against N.C. State. It showed in our performance in Ohio against Kent State, because we were down 25-0 ending the first half. We entered the locker room quietly. Coach Stone came in very mad, so mad that he knocked over a cooler when he walked in, "What is this?" he said. "Did y'all come to play? Did y'all even get on the plane? You all better get it together, because you are embarrassing yourselves and the university. This is not the University of South Alabama football team we know. Where is your heart? There are thirty minutes left in this game. Come out and play." Coach Stone stormed out of the locker room.

We came back in the second half like the South Alabama team we knew we were. Kent state scored on the opening drive after the kickoff to start the half. Our first drive back on offense, Coach Rubble called rip 60 shave; it was double slants. I got in my stance and the quarterback called my name, "Lav! Lav!" When I looked, he was giving me the sluggo signal and I thought, "Oh, snap! Wait, can he do that? Should I run the route? Well, he is the quarterback. He called it. I will run it." He hiked the ball. I came off the ball, one, two and three, and stuck to the slant. Looked in for the slant, one, two, three and broke back to the go. I was wide open. The quarterback launched the ball to me. I made the catch down-field and took off. The safety made a shoestring tackle on me. After that, we scored twenty-five unanswered points but we lost our second-straight game in school history on a last-minute Hail Mary pass play.

We would go on to lose two of the next six games to finish the season at 6-4. When we finished playing our last game I overheard Coach Stone tell Coach Rubble, "You just coached your last game here." "Thank you for the opportunity," Coach Rubble replied. I had never witnessed someone being fired like that. I ran over to Tre and Vernel and said, "Y'all, Coach Rubble just got fired." "Well, bra," Vernel said, "it be like that sometimes." Tre let out a fairly loud chuckle, "Lav, for real?" "Yeah, bra, he said you just coached your last game," I said. "Dang! just like that he has to find a new job." I felt bad for Coach Rubble though because that was a tough way to be fired. However, like I said in the beginning of the season it would be history. It just wasn't the type of history I was expecting. This year's exit meeting with Coach Simp was more encouraging. "Bryant Lavender," Coach Simp said in that meeting, "you grew so much this year. Many people did not expect you to have the type of season that you had, but I knew if you kept your work ethic and stayed hungry to get better that you would have a good season. I am proud of you, because you did that. Continue to get better." I had a huge smile on my face when I said, "Thanks, Coach. Hey, since Coach Rubble is not here anymore are you going to apply for the O.C. position? "I haven't decided that yet, Lav. Why do you ask?" he said. "Well, you told us that your goal was to become an O.C. within the next five years," I said. "This is your opportunity right here. Why not?" Coach Simp smiled and said, "We will see, Lav." I shook his hand, laughed a little and left his office.

Two days later I had my exit meeting with Coach Stone. By then, I was getting used to it. I walked into his office confidently. "Lav, how are you?" he asked. "I'm well, Coach," I said. "How are you?" "I'm good," he said. "Lav, how much are you weighing now?" "I weigh about 185," I said. "Really," he said, "I thought you were about 195. You played strong and big this year, huge improvement from your freshman year." I grinned and said, "Thanks, Coach I have been working." "Really appreciate what you have done here," he said, "and the playmaker you turned into. We have confidence in you and your ability." I sat and listened to what he said and could not help but wonder if he was being honest with me. Most of what he had said was true. I had made tremendous improvement, but I had a hard time believing he was confident in my ability. "Thank you, Coach," I managed to say after he had finished his statements. I shook his hand and walked out of his office thinking, "God, look at what you have done. Look how you have turned everything around for me. The least of men."

Over Christmas break we found out that Coach Simp had accepted a job at Fresno State. I was sad because he was an awesome coach who cared for his players. The best receiver coach I have had since Coach Coe had me in high school. He gave me a call to let me know that he was leaving. I wished him well and told him that I would stay in contact. I thanked him for everything he had done for me. I thanked him for pushing me to be better when I thought I had already reached my ceiling. I thanked him for giving me a legit chance to show what I could do. A few days later we were informed of the new pickups for the staff. A Coach Block from Southern Miss, A Coach Porcell from Memphis and G.A. named Coach Duke would be with the strength and conditioning staff. When we came back for the spring, we met all of them. Coach Block was a high-energy person with a bunch of enthusiasm. He brought a spread offense system with him. It was very similar to what Southern Miss had been running with success. Coach Porcell was a real calm guy, talked well and was highly intelligent with creating plays, and he chewed gum all the time. Coach Duke was my favorite of the new additions to the Jaguar staff. He had played safety at University of Lafayette Louisiana. He was a very driven and relatable person who had a passion to be great. His presence forced you to be great. If you were not great, it was almost disrespectful.

It was a challenge to get the offense on one accord during the spring. There were spurts when we executed the offense perfectly and other times we looked horrible. In our receiver meetings, it was difficult to understand what Porcell and Block wanted because of the amount of changes they consistently made. We knew that they were not on the same page, because of the different ways they said to run routes. During the summer, Coach Duke really got cool with Vernel, Tre and me. He used to come kick it with us. We would talk life, football and joke around. He truly encouraged us to give everything we had every moment. He was the catalyst to giving us a new perspective to certain things. When we wanted to do extra work, he gave us a new drill and pushed us past what we thought we could do. He lifted with us during our workout group. He really added a different dynamic that year to summer weights. Coach Benny always brought a new flare to weights and Coach Duke was just that. We as a group were going through a lot. Tre was dealing with an injury that happened against N.C. State, Vernel was getting pushed all the way to the side at the running back position. He never really had an honest shot. I could feel the confidence they claimed to have disappearing right before my very eyes.

Before the summer was over Vernel came to me and said, "Yo, Lav, I don't think I want to play football anymore. I just do not have a love for the game anymore." "What is wrong, bro?" I replied. "Man, I was sitting here thinking, I am tired, bra. I am tired of them treating me like a scrub. Lav, I am not sorry," he said. "I know, bra, you are a beast. Just see this season through, bra, we started together," I encouraged him. "I don't know if I can see this through man," he answered. I went to get the Bible and came back and said, "Remember what the Bible says in Romans 8:28, everything is going to work out for your good, bra." He looked at me with tears coming down his face, "Lav, it was not supposed to be like this." I flipped to another scripture and said, "I know, bra, but look in Matthew 19:30 it says, 'But many who are first will be last and many who are last will be first. Bra, do not quit right now. God is preparing you for your destiny. At least finish this year with Tre and me." He wiped his tears away and nodded at my suggestion. Tre came in the room from treatment and said, "Fellas, we need to have a room meeting." We all found a spot in the living room, and we all knew we were about to have a heart-to-heart. Tre went first and said, "They said I need surgery because there are small pieces of bones loose in my knee. I will miss all of camp and the first two games. I do not think I will play that much because when I come back I will be out of shape. I am going to do the surgery because if I prolong it I could make it worse. I want to be able to walk after I get done playing football." Vernel went next and said, "Tre, I just told Lav that I don't want to play anymore for real. This will be my last year playing with y'all most likely. I know I will not get any burn at running back, but I will definitely hold down the special teams." "Well, Lav, it's up to you to hold it down for 1814 this year. May the force be with you, my black brother." We all laughed at Tre's statement, but I honestly felt the weight from what had just taken place. That season had not started and already it felt different. My two roommates had been there for me since I got to South Alabama; they had always had a positive mindset. To see them worn, tired and hurt did something to me on the inside. We had shed blood, sweat and tears, literally, with each other.

REDSHIRT JUNIOR YEAR

Fall came and it was not fun at all. Tre could not practice, and Vernel was done with everybody. We did have fun, though, when we had a chance to rest before the next period started. There was pressure on everyone because of the schedule that year. It was a full FBS schedule. The other years, we did not have an FBS schedule, because we were a first-year program my freshman year 2009, and the NCAA made us go through a building process on our schedule before we were officially a member of the Sunbelt conference. We had a thirteen-game schedule, one bye week and new coaches for offense, offensive coordinator and receivers. It was just going to be a tough year. During camp I could tell they were trying to repeat what had happened to me freshman year. Except, I was too valuable to the team. They could not sideline me. I learned the offense, and I was executing efficiently. At one time, they had confidence in my ability, but that went away when I started to notice them taking me out of deep routes. If I happened to run a deep route, I was the decoy. I did play in every game, and had a majority of the snaps, but most of the time I just ran sprints in a game. I only remember being involved in two games the whole year and those were against Mississippi State University and Hawaii. In the MSU game, I finished with six catches for eighty yards. After that big game I thought for sure they would incorporate me into the offensive scheme, but they always said do not put your faith in one man. There was no change. I felt so disrespected. I stopped smiling, talking and laughing at practice. It was the only way I knew how not to kick the bucket over. Every day I just thought about what Coach Simp had said when we spoke back in the summer of 2010. Just about every Coach came up to me and asked, "Lav, what is wrong? I have noticed you have not been smiling or laughing at practice that is not like you. Is something going on at home? Is something going on with your girlfriend? Is it your classes? If there is something I can do to help please talk to me so I can help." I replied, "Nothing is wrong outside of football. Everything other than football is great." I said that to every coach who asked me those questions. I wanted to express myself to them, but I did not trust the ones who asked me. They might use what I said against me, so I kept my mouth shut and did my job. The coaches who did not ask me already knew what was going on and felt the same way I did. I finally broke my silence in Hawaii. We had a turnover on downs on a back-to-back series and I lashed out just a little bit. Coach Porcell was pacing the sideline and I yelled out, "Coach, Porcell! Throw me the freaking ball! I can go deep, too!" He looked at me, might have been a little shocked, but he nodded his head. I cut my eyes to look away, and I found myself locking eyes with the quarterback. I nodded my head at him and he nodded back. I finished the game with three catches for 150 yards, but due to flags on the play in the stat book, only one catch for twenty-six yards was recorded.

We finished the season 2-11. Such a disappointing season it was, when we got back from Hawaii I looked up toward the sky and said, "God, please give me the words to say for this exit meeting. I do not want to say something I will regret." I had set my exit meeting with Coach Porcell on Monday so I could get it over. I knocked on the door. "Lav, come in," he said. I walked in, sat down and waited for him to start talking. "Lav, you had solid year for us, make sure that you are in the best shape possible, because it looked like you got tired toward the second half of the season. This year coming up we need you to have more games like you had against Mississippi State and Hawaii. We need maximum production from you in this year coming up," he said. "First off, Coach, I was tired," I said. "I am playing sixty-five to seventy snaps a game and just running go routes. I'm expected to run full speed and I don't even get a ball thrown to me on the go route. In order for me to produce the way, I did against Mississippi State and Hawaii I need to be in the read." "What do you mean?" he asked. "How can I give you those types of games when you tell the quarterback not to look my way?" I said. "It is not possible when he is not looking at me as an option to throw the ball to. It is a lot on someone to know you have seventy snaps and you may get three targets from the quarterback, when in the past you have had high production." "Lav," Coach said, "we will do a better job of rotating the receivers to keep everyone fresh." I knew, in other words, that they just could use something against me and replace me with who they really wanted at the X-receiver. I walked out of his office and looked up to the sky as I walked out of the field house and said, "God, I told the truth. I was played this season for real, but I did not kick the bucket over. I know You will work it out for me. Whatever you need me to be for my team I will be." I finished my statement and walked back to my room with that weight lifted off my shoulders.

When I walked in Coach Stone's office for the exit interview, it was a little different than previous years. It was the last time I would be evaluated for an upcoming season. After next season, I would be done playing for South. He opened up with, "Bryant Lavender, thank you for everything you have done here. I am proud of you." "Thank you, Coach," I said, "for giving me the opportunity to play here and to be a part of history." "Lav," he said, "you graduate this May, right? Are you coming back for your fifth year?" He had a curious look. "Yes, sir," I said, "I do, and yes, I am coming back." "That is exciting," he said with a smile. "I remember when I graduated. Is all your family planning on coming?" He said with a smile. I smiled while answering, "Yes, that is the plan." "Well, Bryant, anything I can ever help you with just let me know," he assured me. "Yes sir. Thank you," I said shaking his hand and walking out of the office.

When I got home for Christmas break I went to see Coach Coe as I always did. He asked a ton of questions, "Bryant," he said, "why didn't they throw you the ball like they have over the last few years? You were open most of the time and the other times you were blocking. What is up with that?" "I was not in the read, Coach. I was the decoy route," I answered. "Decoy route? The ones that were thrown to were double-covered most of the time," he said with a confused look. "Well, you know, Coach, teams watch film, too, so they knew I was not getting the ball," I replied with a nonchalant look. "Why hasn't Stone stepped in and said something?" he asked. "Coach, I do not know." He looked at me with a disgruntled face and said, "What do you mean you do not know? You have been faithful to South Alabama. You have done everything they have asked you after they did not feel like you were a player. You have proved yourself time and time again, what more do they need?" I had a blank face, "Coach, if I knew," I said, "I would have done it already." I knew Coach Coe had more questions but he could see that I was beginning to get a little frustrated with trying to answer his questions that I did not have answers for. He finished the conversation off with, "Well, you will at least get a great education and a degree out of the deal." All I could do was laugh at the last statement. No matter what, I knew he had my back.

In the spring, we knew Vernel was not coming back to football, so during football it was just Tre and me going to weights. Vernel and I were graduating with our bachelor's degrees in May, so we saw each other a lot for that because we had to do many of the same things. Our first football meeting in the spring was very different, that year. We were on the front row signifying that we were seniors. As we were waiting on Coach Stone to come in and address the team, Tre leaned over to me and said, "Lav, you know you getting number five." I shook my head no and said, "Naw, bra, I do not want it. Let them give it to someone else," I said. "Who, Lav? You are the only one that fits the description of someone who gets that award. You might as well get ready," he said confidently.

The number five belonged to a teammate of ours who had passed away in a motorcycle accident. He was the epitome of what you wanted in a player, teammate and a friend. He was one person who wanted you to do well and pushed you to the limit. He did everything right on and off the field even while going through adversity. I, Bryant Lavender, did not know if I could or had the ability to represent him or his number well. I had so much respect for my big brother. I was afraid I might not live up to the greatness he possessed.

Coach Stone finally came in to address the team, "Everyone, it is time to get the 2013 season under way, and it starts now with this preparation. Everyone buy in now so we can have success later on in the season. No excuses, just work to achieve the goal at hand. The goal is to be the best in the Sunbelt. The goal is set, now let's go out and be that. Make sure everyone knows and respects who we are. You all know that we give number five to the senior who exemplifies everything we expect you to be. The senior who does the right thing on and off the field, a leader, someone we can trust. The person we chose this year to wear number five – and, when his name came up it was a unanimous decision. . ." The whole time I was thinking, "Please don't call my name. Please don't call my name" -- "...Bryant Lavender," Coach Stone said my name. I just sat there for three seconds, I did not move until Tre hit me on my shoulder. I stood up, shook Coach Stone's hand and turned to face the team. They were waiting for me to say something. As I scanned the room from the front to the back all I could muster was, "Time to go to work," and took my seat. There was no hiding now; this publicly established me as the leader with the presentation of number five. I guess God just told me what my team needed me to be.

Coach Porcell kept his word and found a receiver that would replace me. In the spring, I saw it happening. I was not worried too much because I knew I would play. I was just wondering if he would mess me over on pass plays. After all, this would be the last of everything I would be able to do for the program as far as contributing my physical ability. God allowed me to have a great spring for football. I passed the GRE for graduate school, and I walked across the stage, receiving a bachelor's degree in exercise science. Everything was going according to plan. Next thing on my mind was setting everything up for the NFL.

REDSHIRT SENIOR YEAR

Right before the season started, they released some pictures I had had taken back in the spring. I did not think anything of it. I thought it was going in the programs for that year. Little did I know it would be everywhere. It was on billboards, in the mall, on the city buses, and plastered all over the stadium. The picture they used was with my arm stretched out, my mouth opened, and with my new jersey number five. The way the picture turned out was amazing. In my mind what made it the perfect fit was it was the fifth year the program had been in existence. I was getting texts, calls and tags on social media from everyone. I was not mentally prepared for how that picture turned out or how enormous an impact it would have on the city. God had a master plan and He still was working it out before my very eyes.

As the season started, it was tough for me because I did not play as I expected to. I only went in for blocking plays. In the first three games, I had one catch for six yards. I knew that everything I said to Coach Porcell was coming back to me. All I could do was ask God, "Is this what you need me to be?" I did not agree with sitting on the bench. The fourth game we played the University of Tennessee on ESPN 2. During the game, I spoke to God out loud, "God, I know my senior year is not going to finish like this. I have been too faithful for it to end like this." I finished the game with four catches for fifty-five yards. God heard my petition and He changed things in my favor. As the season progressed we were in the hunt for bowl eligibility, and I saw less and less playing time. When we played University of Louisiana-Monroe, I was only seeing action on special teams. When the third quarter came around, I began to get discouraged and mentally checked out of the game because I was not going to get in on offense. Tre looked over and yelled, "Lav, stay in the game." I gave him a "whatever look" and unbuckled my chinstrap. He repeated his statement, "Lav, stay in the game." This time when he said it, I realized it was God talking to me. "I will stay in the game for one more series," I thought. On the next offensive series, my teammate who had been put over me went down with a torn Achilles tendon. They were forced to use Tre and me for the rest of that game and for the rest of the season. We finished bowl eligible with a record of 6-6, but we were not selected for a bowl. Mentally checking out of that game would have been symbolizing me checking out on God. I am thankful that God sent me a warning twice.

When I went to clean out my locker for good, I found a letter addressed to me from Coach Stone. It read, "Bryant, you are one heck of a great person, you have true character, you are a competitor and most of all, people can trust you. Thanks for being here at South. You are one of the builders of this program, and you did it the right way." Before we went on Christmas break I wanted to meet with Coach Stone to see if he still would be willing to help me like he said just a year ago. I specifically wanted to ask how he could help me do anything to get an opportunity in the NFL. I walked into his office and said, "Hey, Coach, how are you doing?" "I am good," he said. "How are you?" "I am well, Coach," I said. "I was wondering if you could help me with something" I was a little nervous. "Bryant," he said, "you know I would be more than glad to help you. Do you need help looking for a job? Do you a recommendation letter?" I smiled and said, "No, not that yet. You know I am going to train for the NFL." "Oh yeah? That's right," he said and I looked at him and thought, "Did he just try and play me?" "Well, Bryant," he said, "if you ever need help with anything or need me to connect you to someone I know that can help you just let me know. I know a lot of people that are looking for former football players to work for them." "Well, Coach, that's what I was coming to ask your help for. Anything you do to help connect me to an agent or recommend one that would be great," I said. "Oh yeah," he said, "that, too." I knew from that statement was not going to help me. I left his office, and I went to Coach Benny's office. I opened the door and said, "Coach, Benny, I need your help to get to the league. I am not going to get any special trainer. You know my strengths and my weaknesses. I have been with you for five years, I trust you." He said, "Brother, you know I will. I will have a pro day training program ready when you come back from Christmas break." "Thanks, Coach," I said. I walked out of his office determined that I would surprise people on March 7, 2014.

When I came back in the spring, Coach Benny handed me a packet and explained everything to me. It was head down, feet running. I trained four days, twice a day, and ran three days out of the week. I received directions from him on weights, Coach Ron for abs and Coach Mak for my sprint mechanics. For nine weeks, I put in the work to make sure I was ready. I was going to perform to my top potential. These three individuals played an amazing part in my preparation for pro day. Two weeks from pro-day, Coach Mak had me run four forties to find out how many I needed to run before I got on the actual clock. He wanted us to know when our fastest forty would happen. My first two forties were 4.5, but when I ran, my third one Coach Mak threw the stopwatch to me and it read, 4.47. On the fourth one, he did the same thing and it read 4.48. That was the first time in my life I had clocked a 4.4. After finishing, I looked at Coach Mak and said, "Coach, I am running a low 4.4 come pro-day." He smiled and replied, "I will be waiting on it." I got curious to the number receivers that were coming out with me, so I looked it up. When I looked at the total number of receivers entering the draft there was 325. Among them, I ranked 300. That was awful, but after my pro-day, that would change.

Coach Coe called me the night before pro-day and said, "Bryant, you have been waiting for this moment to come. This is what you train for. This is why you have spent countless hours perfecting your craft. Do what you have been coached to do. Perform at the high level we know you can." I smiled and said, "Yes, sir. Coach, are you coming to watch? You know you have been there for every big football event since high school."

"Well, Bryant," he said, "I think you should experience this yourself. I don't want to distract you. I want you to pay attention to them. I will wait for your phone call." "OK, Coach, thanks for everything. I love you," I said with a smile. "I love you too, buddy," he said. "Call me when you get done." As soon as I get off the phone with him, Pastor Gee called me and said, "Hey there, son. What time does your pro-day start tomorrow?" I smiled and said, "It starts at two p.m." "All right. We will be there," he said confidently. "Really?" I asked surprised. "Yeah, son. We are going to make that happen. Remember to run like no one is watching but God," he said. "Yes, sir," I replied.

The next day I got to the field house early, and the scouts instructed us to go into the defensive lineman meeting room. The teams represented were Steelers, Colts, Seahawks, Dolphins, Saints and Broncos. Before we took the Wonderlic IQ test the Steelers scout said, "From here on out, you are competing for a game-day check. This is your chance to catch our attention, so catch it. The league minimum for a game day check averages about $400,000. If you sign on the practice squad, your check will clear $5,500 every Tuesday. So, good luck to you all." That was when the Seahawk's scout brought in the tests and said, "When you get done, go to the weight room." When I finished I went to the weight room and was instructed to go get my height and weight recorded. The Colts scout took my height and said, "51007." I weighed in at 183 pounds. The Seahawk scout got my wingspan, and said, "72 inches." He also did my hand size, it was 10.1, and from there I went to vertical jump, 41 inches. I jumped 10 feet, 2 inches in the broad. I had 10 feet, 4 inches, but I fell. Next, I had to bench press, I did not know how well I was going to do on that. It was either a hit or miss for me. Coach B was calling out our reps when I got to rep four I racked the weight because I knew I would not be successful on anymore reps. He looked at me and said, "Bryant Lavender, four reps," with a disappointing tone of voice. I hit my chest twice and yelled, "Field work!" I went over to get my book bag that was two power racks down. Coach Stone come out of nowhere, "Lav, what do you think you will run in the forty?" I stared him in the eyes and said, "I am going to run a four, four." He responds, "four, four-nine." I stared in his eyes again and said, "I am going to run faster than that." He looked at me and said, "Four, four-eight." I giggled a little bit, looked him in the eyes one last time and said, "I will run faster than that, too." "All right, we will see," he retorted as I threw my book bag strap over my shoulder.

As I walked up the hill, I saw my pastor, first lady and a few other members from my church walking up the hill. I stopped and gave them hugs and went to warm-up. As I got ready to run the forty, all I could think about was running to save my father's life. I stepped up to the line, took a deep breath, set my feet, stretched out, curled back, got set and exploded off the line. The whole time thinking, "Go get your Dad. Save your Dad." I flew past the forty-yard line and noticed out of my peripheral view the scouts head followed me. Walking back to the starting line to wait my turn, I heard my teammate call my name, "Lav!" and put up four, three and seven with his fingers. I said, "What!" he nodded and repeated the hand signal. I ran over to Coach Mak, "Coach, what did you get?" I asked. He threw me the stopwatch and it read, 4.39. All I did was look up and said, "God, let your will be done." When it was my turn to run again I repeated everything. Before I took off I said, "Here we go, Daddy." After I flew past the line again, another teammate called my name, "Lav, that was four, four-zero good run." I nodded to him and pointed to God. After the rest of the testing, they separated us by offense and defense. We ran about seven routes. I had one drop on the curl route. Overall, it was a great day for me. God showed up and showed out.

When they released us, the Seahawk scout called me back and said, "Bryant, do you have a highlight tape I can watch?" "Yes, sir," I said, "I have two on YouTube. You see one with me wearing number eight and one of me wearing number five. I am going to let you know now that I was the third-down man. I was not the go-to receiver, but I made plays when they came my way," I said openly. He smiled and said, "That is perfect, and that is what we are looking for, a workhorse. Thank you for being honest. Also, is there film on you in the field house where we can watch the games?" I noticed the Dolphins scout behind him writing things down as well. "Yes, sir," I said, "they have all the film in the field house." "OK," he said, "thanks, Bryant." I began to jog off the field, then I stopped and turned back, "The reason my number changed was because I received the senior award." He turned and wrote that down on his pad, "Bryant, that is awesome," he replied.

The following week I went back to the check my ranking. Now out of the 325 receivers coming out with me, I ranked 129. I went to the field house to finish out the workout program Coach Benny had created for me when the players and a few coaches came in and congratulated me on a great pro-day. I was confused because I had not told anybody about what I had done. I found out by my quarterback that Coach Stone said this to the team, "You have to have that determination and work ethic like Bryant Lavender. If you had told me that he would run a four, four-five in the forty, I would not believe you. On his, pro-day he told me he would run a four, four, and I really did not believe him. But he did. He ran a four, four-five in the forty." He had said that after the first day of spring practice. The reason it was a four, four-five was because we did not have the laser machine working when they tested us.

Later that week my phone rang from an unknown number, "Hello," I said. "Hello, is this Bryant Lavender?" the voice on the line said. "Yes, this is he," I answered, wondering who this was. "This is Stan Flemington with the Miami Dolphins; do you have a few minutes to talk?" My face lit up, I jumped up and down before I answered his question, "Yes, sir, I do."

Question

Do you believe you are chosen by God?

"Remember, I was not the athlete they thought they signed. I was however, the athlete God chose."

93691430R00068

Made in the USA
Columbia, SC
13 April 2018